LOST
BOOK
OF
SPELLS

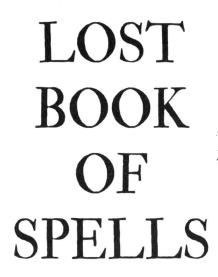

LOST
BOOK
OF
SPELLS

FIONA HORNE

ROCKPOOL

A Rockpool book
PO Box 252
Summer Hill
NSW 2130
Australia

rockpoolpublishing.com
Follow us! f ☺ rockpoolpublishing
Tag your images with #rockpoolpublishing

ISBN: 9781922786005

Published in 2025 by Rockpool Publishing

Caution: always check with your medical practitioner before using any
herb if you are pregnant, breastfeeding, or have a medical condition.

Design and typesetting by Sara Lindberg, Rockpool Publishing
Edited by Jess Cox

 A catalogue record for this
book is available from the
National Library of Australia

Printed and bound in China
10 9 8 7 6 5 4 3 2 1

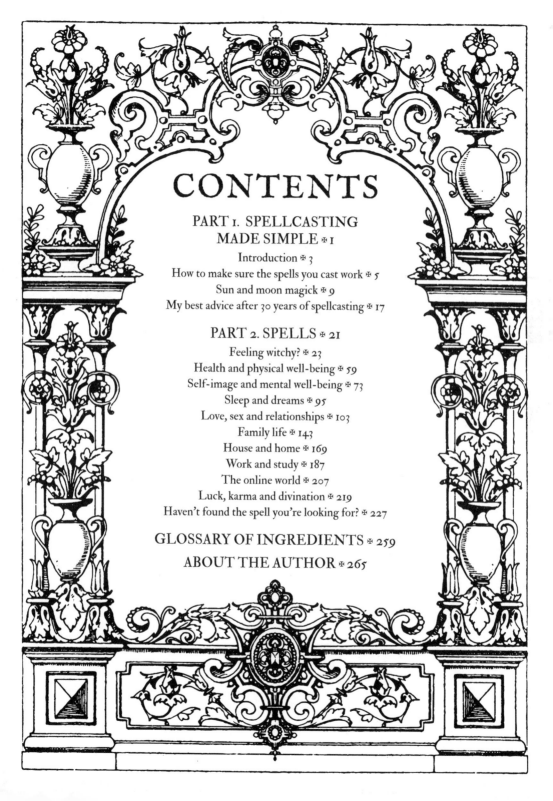

CONTENTS

PART I.

SPELL-CASTING MADE SIMPLE

INTRODUCTION

You might think a lost book of spells would be uncovered from under a pile of rocks in the ruins of an ancient temple ... but these days it could be a lost computer file!

On the original version of my website, fionahorne.com, which I created back in the 1990s with the help of two wonderful girls, Tracey and Lauren, I had a *Spell Book* with 170 spells covering all sorts of everyday needs and wishes. When I rebuilt my website in the early 2000s, the spell book was deleted ... gone forever, I thought. But all these years later, I found it buried in the depths of the internet! Well, actually it was my dear friend Michael Herkes, aka The Glam Witch, who did the hunting and found it!

The original *Spell Book* was the result of two years I spent as a 'resident radio witch' on Australia's top easy-listening station, MIX 101 FM's *The Morning Show with Richard Stubbs*.

Listeners called in requesting spells for many different problems and situations - and I was charged with solving them live on the radio! Richard is a gifted comedian, and we always had a good laugh over many situations but also gave listeners serious solutions. The feedback I received on the effectiveness of these spells was overwhelmingly positive. Over the years, so many people have asked me if I could reinstate the *Spell Book*. Because of its origins, it's a unique collection of magickal advice addressing the needs of everyday people.

Since those days, I've written and prescribed many more spells, addressing the evolving experience of life on this planet. Not only am I reviewing and updating the original spells, I'm adding more spells that address social media challenges, environmental concerns, privacy, autonomy and more ... for love, money and health in this busy, convoluted world!

You are welcome to browse through this book and get stuck into casting spells for positive change or perhaps first take a moment to review the next few pages, which offer my best advice on casting spells that can really work.

Remember, the best tool for making magick happen is closer than you think - it's in your own mind and heart. It's in your ability to put aside disbelief, cynicism and fear, and allow yourself to consider that something extraordinary is possible! Your best spellcasting asset is the belief that there really is magick in the universe and you can co-create your reality with it.

HOW TO MAKE SURE THE SPELLS YOU CAST WORK

The key to unlocking magick in your life is to have a relationship with magick: to co-create with the universe.

When you cast the spells offered in this book, follow the instructions to the best of your ability. If you feel inspired to do things a little differently (for instance, instead of doing a spell during the full moon, you feel inspired to perform it at sunrise), let your intuition guide you. Don't be afraid to put your own stamp on a spell authentically and enthusiastically, as long as you're not being lazy or apathetic, like if you think: *Oh, this won't work, I'll leave this bit out. What does it matter?* That's not your intuition guiding you, that's your self-doubt being an obstacle! Push it aside and get unapologetically confident!

If you're having trouble sourcing certain items, I have a section on substitutions you can make to help you along (see Substituting ingredients, page 7). But try to stick to the original spell as much as you can. You wouldn't follow a chocolate cake recipe, decide to swap the cocoa for vanilla and still expect it to taste like chocolate, would you?

CREATING A SACRED SPACE TO MAKE MAGICK

Standing in the centre of your chosen space to work magick, stand with your finger pointing outwards and turn around slowly, tracing a circle as you say:

I conjure thee circle,
The gate of enlightenment,
A space of enchantment.
Above and below,
Light around me,
Light within me.

Another way you can create a sacred space is to do a smudging ritual.

HOW TO PERFORM A SMUDGING RITUAL

Smudging a room clears away negative energies. You do this by burning sage or other incense. Carry the burning sage or incense around the room, pausing at each corner. Then using your hand or a feather, wave the smoke deeper into the corners.

Before smudging, light a white candle to invoke the positive cleansing energies of the fire element for clearing away negative energies and obstacles.

When you feel the space is cleansed and aligned, place your smudging implement in a fireproof dish and leave it burning throughout your ritual or spellcasting. Snuff it out when your work is complete.

An old Hungarian bedtime charm is to check the corners of your room before sleeping. They believed if harmful spirits were going to gather anywhere it would be the corners of rooms. So

give these areas an extra cleansing release to affirm that only positive, constructive energies can inhabit your magickal space.

SUBSTITUTING INGREDIENTS

When practising magick, flexibility and creativity are key. Sometimes, we may find ourselves without the exact ingredients a spell recipe calls for. However, this presents an opportunity to tap into our intuition and resourcefulness. Instead of feeling discouraged, we can embrace the magick of substitution, knowing that the intention behind our spell is what truly matters.

Whether we use herbs from our kitchen, stones found in nature or even symbolic representations, we can infuse our spells with personal energy and meaning. By trusting in our intuition and the power of intention, we can create spells that are uniquely ours, filled with positivity and potency. After all, while every ingredient suggested in these spells is aligned with our magickal goal and intention; the deepest magick flows not from the ingredients themselves but from the energy and intention we imbue into our craft.

In these days of instant gratification and online shopping, it can be tempting to just buy things from all over the world and have them shipped to you. But think about the carbon footprint you are making. How many times is an item irradiated as it travels through different time zones and across borders? If you can make your substitution from a locally sourced item, you'll have something ideal and more powerful. Research the qualities of the herbs and crystals or items you need, and find something local that is similar. Your intention will align the magick to its most powerful effect.

TIPS ON CANDLE MAGICK

Candle magick is featured a lot in this book. Lighting coloured candles, burning candles, carving symbols into candles ... they have so many uses!

Over the years, I've found that choosing candles in a mindful, conscious way is helpful to empower your spells and ensure good results. Use candles made from non-harmful, non-toxic wax; coloured with non-chemical dyes; and scented with essential oils and non-toxic perfumes.

If you want to align your energies most potently, make your own candles or join with other witches where you each have a task - one is the candlemaker, one is the herb grower, one is the pouch sewer ... a witch collective can make spell work easy and energetically empowered. Remember, your magickal concerns are worth more than a quick fix - make the effort to empower your magick mindfully, respectfully and eco-consciously.

SUN AND MOON MAGICK

MOON MAGICK

The phases of the moon hold a profound significance in the practice of spellcasting and ritual, serving as celestial guides to harness and align with the universe's natural rhythms and our place within it.

As the moon waxes and wanes, each phase carries its own energy and symbolism. The waxing phase - as the moon grows from new to full - symbolises manifestation, growth and abundance. This is an ideal time for spells aimed at attracting positivity, setting intentions and manifesting goals.

Conversely, the waning phase - as the moon decreases from full to dark - embodies release, banishment and letting go. This provides an opportunity to shed old patterns, cleanse negative energies and break free from obstacles.

By aligning our practices with the moon's phases, we tap into the inherent power of lunar energies, enhancing the potency and effectiveness of our spells and rituals. With each lunar cycle, we embark on a journey of transformation, renewal and spiritual growth guided by the moon's luminous dance in the night sky.

MOON CHART

This magical chart outlines suggested activities, intentions and corresponding spellcasting practices for each phase of the moon to enchant your magickal life.

New moon

ACTIVITIES	Setting intentions, planting seeds for new beginnings, cleansing rituals
INTENTIONS	Fresh starts, new opportunities, initiating projects, setting goals
SPELLCASTING PRACTICES	Visualisation exercises, intention-setting rituals, manifestation spells, charging objects with energy

Waxing crescent

ACTIVITIES	Nurturing intentions, gathering resources, taking inspired action
INTENTIONS	Growth, expansion, development, attracting abundance
SPELLCASTING PRACTICES	Candle magick for growth and abundance, prosperity spells, goal-setting rituals, charging crystals

First quarter

ACTIVITIES	Overcoming challenges, taking decisive action, building momentum
INTENTIONS	Breaking through obstacles, making progress, empowerment
SPELLCASTING PRACTICES	Protection spells, courage rituals, spells for clarity and focus, energy work

Waxing gibbous

ACTIVITIES	Refining plans, fine-tuning intentions, staying focused
INTENTIONS	Refinement, optimisation, preparation for manifestation
SPELLCASTING PRACTICES	Spell work for success and achievement, manifestation rituals, charging spell tools

Full moon

ACTIVITIES	Celebration, illumination, supercharging all spellcasting efforts. Many spells come to fruition on the full moon. This is a great time to do rituals of gratitude for what you have and share your abundant energy out into the world in a gesture of unconditional goodwill and love.
INTENTIONS	Completion, fulfilment, manifestation, supercharging, gratitude
SPELLCASTING PRACTICES	Full moon rituals, charging objects under moonlight, gratitude ceremonies, divination

Waning gibbous

ACTIVITIES	Reflecting on progress, integrating lessons learned, preparing for closure
INTENTIONS	Letting go, releasing, clearing away obstacles
SPELLCASTING PRACTICES	Banishing spells, breaking bad habits, releasing rituals, forgiveness ceremonies

Last quarter

ACTIVITIES	Evaluating progress, tying up loose ends, making space for new opportunities
INTENTIONS	Closure, endings, completion, reflection
SPELLCASTING PRACTICES	Cord-cutting rituals, closure ceremonies, releasing attachments, gratitude spells

Waning crescent

ACTIVITIES	Resting, recharging, inner reflection, preparing for the next cycle
INTENTIONS	Rest, introspection, surrender, self-care
SPELLCASTING PRACTICES	Dreamwork, meditation, energy cleansing, purification rituals

Dark moon

ACTIVITIES	A magickal time of rest, good for divination and honouring ancestors and spirits

By aligning your spellcasting and ritual practices with the moon's phases, you can enhance your magick's potency and effectiveness, harnessing the natural energies of the lunar cycle to support your intentions and goals.

SUN MAGICK

Working with the energies of the sun in ritual and spellcasting is an incredibly uplifting and empowering experience. The sun is a symbol of vitality, strength and enlightenment, serving as a beacon of divine energy that fuels our intentions and manifestations.

We can draw inspiration from Ra, the original Egyptian sun god, to add a profound layer of wisdom and mysticism to our practices. In ancient Egypt, Ra was revered as the giver of life, representing the ultimate source of power and creation.

By tapping into this ancient lineage, we honour the rich heritage of human spirituality and connect with the timeless essence of the known and unknown universe. Modern magick and spells often find their roots in the sacred traditions of ancient Egypt, when practitioners worked intimately with the natural elements and celestial bodies to weave spells of protection, healing and transformation. (For more, see Egyptian spells, pages 243–246.) Incorporating these age-old techniques into our own rituals lets us harness the radiant energy of the sun to illuminate our paths and manifest our desires with clarity and purpose. By embracing the sun's warmth and brilliance we step into our own divine potential, embarking on a journey of spiritual awakening and personal growth.

SUN CHART

The following chart outlines the phases of the sun throughout the day and notes some activities for spellcasting and ritual during each phase. Feel free to adapt these suggestions to suit your own personal practices and intentions.

PHASE OF THE SUN	TIME OF DAY	SPELLCASTING/RITUAL ACTIVITIES
Sunrise	Dawn	Setting intentions for the day, purification
Morning	Late morning	Spell work for new beginnings, growth, creativity
Noon	Midday	Empowerment rituals, energy work, manifestation
Afternoon	Afternoon	Healing rituals, meditation, gratitude practice
Sunset	Dusk	Release rituals, letting go of negativity, reflection
Twilight	Evening	Divination, connecting with spirit guides, dream work
Night	Late evening	Protection rituals, ancestor veneration, astral projection

DEOSIL AND WIDDERSHINS ... WHAT?

These two witchy words relate to the movement of the sun across the sky. Deosil means 'with the sun' and is associated with the concepts of growth, expansion and manifestation. Widdershins means 'against the sun' and represents the ideas of banishing, releasing and introspection. The practice of casting spells is influenced by the perceived movement of the sun across the sky, which in turn affects the interpretation of directional movement in your rituals.

In the northern hemisphere, the sun appears to veer south as it travels from east to west across the sky, in a clockwise direction. Conversely, in the southern hemisphere, the sun appears to veer north on its path in an anticlockwise direction. Put simply, if clocks were invented in the southern hemisphere, the arms would move in the opposite direction to how they currently move!

Therefore, in the northern hemisphere deosil is clockwise, but is anticlockwise in the southern hemisphere. Similarly, widdershins is anticlockwise in the northern hemisphere, but is clockwise in the southern hemisphere. But while the directional movement may seem reversed in the two hemispheres, the symbolic meanings remain consistent. The difference in casting spells between the hemispheres lies in how deosil and widdershins are interpreted based on the perceived movement of the sun across the sky. Magickal practitioners adapt their rituals to align with their geographical location and corresponding solar observations.

To keep it simple and confidently potent for you, in this book I'll say 'clockwise in the north and anticlockwise in the south'. You'll see!

MY BEST ADVICE AFTER 30 YEARS OF SPELLCASTING

When our spells seem to fail, how can we ask the universe to lend a hand in crafting our life to be more magickal than our dreams and projections? If we've got shelves full of spell books, we love making charms and lighting candles, and we pour our sincere intentions and efforts into our craft every time ... yet find our magickal efforts falling short, it might be time to switch our thinking and refresh our relationship with our craft.

Here's the secret: stop asking for things just for you and start helping others instead.

Instead of spending time casting spells, try something different for a while. Do small rituals to show gratitude and respect for the earth and everyone around you. This kind of magic isn't about control - it's about trusting that good things will come to you when you're ready for them. And you know what? It usually brings better experiences and opportunities than you could have asked for.

When we're young, our ego helps us figure out who we are and where we fit in. But as we grow older, it can get in the way. So, try to let go of the need to control everything with spells, including the universe. I know that may sound strange when you're sitting here holding this spell book! But it's all about balance. The spells aren't going anywhere, they will be here when you're ready. Maybe it's time to read up on the rituals of gratitude and healing in this book and perform those (see Group ritual of gratitude, page 250 and Earth healing ritual, page 253).

When you are working to empower your life after a series of setbacks, instead of trying to micromanage your life with spells that take up a lot of time and energy, keep things simple. Be grateful for what you have right now. Trust me, when you stop trying to control everything, amazing things can start to happen.

In this way of being magickal, we focus on being honest with ourselves and others. We're happy just being ourselves without any conditions or expectations. This kind of magick is all about humility and authenticity, and it's extremely powerful.

Let's leave the old-school way of doing magick behind. Instead of letting our egos take the lead, let's be willing to serve others and do the work that needs to be done. Because when we do, we'll experience a magickal life that's more powerful than we ever thought possible.

PART 2.

SPELLS

FEELING
WITCHY?

RAINBOWS

Are rainbows really good luck? Absolutely! Rainbows carry the full light spectrum and are charged with visible healing and transformative powers. They are the fusion of two of the most transformative elements, water and fire, and are visually awe-inspiring too.

In the *Book of Secrets* (as reported in Paul Beyerl's *Herbal Magick*), Albertus Magnus reveals this magickal formula for conjuring rainbows (and thunderstorms for that matter). Mix the ashes of a cremated snake with dried sage and throw it into the air as you call on a rainbow. One should appear! (Or maybe a 'Rainbow Serpent' of Australian Aboriginal lore).

If you see the full arc of a rainbow, make a wish and it will surely be granted. If the rainbow fades to a partial arc as you do this, your wish is misguided or misplaced. Rainbow blessings can enter your life by surrounding yourself with the seven colours of the light spectrum: red, orange, yellow, green, blue, indigo and violet.

Here is more magickal folklore about rainbows:

BRIDGE TO OTHER WORLDS	In many cultures, rainbows are seen as bridges between the earthly realm and the heavens or other supernatural realms. Crossing a rainbow could lead you into another world or bring good fortune.
POT OF GOLD	One of the most famous myths about rainbows is the pot of gold at the end of a rainbow. According to Celtic folklore, leprechauns hide their pots of gold at the rainbow's end, but this gold is elusive and can never be captured.
RAINBOW SERPENTS	In Aboriginal Australian mythology, rainbows are often associated with a powerful deity known as the Rainbow Serpent. This serpent is the creator responsible for shaping the landscape and controlling water.

RAINBOW AS A SYMBOL OF PROMISE	In Judeo-Christian tradition, the rainbow is a symbol of God's promise to never again flood the earth. It appears in the story of Noah's ark as a covenant between God and humanity.
RAINBOW WARRIORS	Some Native American tribes believe in the prophecy of the rainbow warriors, who are said to bring unity, healing and peace to the world. The rainbow warriors are spiritual leaders who will guide humanity through challenging times.
HEALING POWERS	In various cultures, rainbows are associated with healing and rejuvenation. They believe standing beneath a rainbow or drinking water touched by a rainbow can bring physical or spiritual healing.
LUCK AND PROTECTION	Many people believe that encountering a rainbow brings good luck and protection from harm. In some cultures, it's considered fortunate to see a rainbow before embarking on a journey or making an important decision.
RAINBOW AS A SYMBOL OF DIVERSITY AND INCLUSION	In modern times, the rainbow has become a symbol of diversity, inclusion and LGBTQIA+ pride. It represents the beauty of differences coming together to create something vibrant and harmonious.

These examples of the folklore surrounding rainbows showcase the universal fascination and wonder this magickal projection of light inspires.

FULL MOON MEDITATION

During the full moon, the earth is poised magickally between the moon and sun, and the world is bathed in psychic energy.

1. Light a silver candle and use an oil burner to infuse a few drops of chamomile oil (or geranium or jasmine). Dress in something magickal and white. Using your fingers or a feather, douse your meditation area in moon water (see How to make moon water, following).

2. Lie down and place cucumber slices on your eyelids (for psychic vision). Call on the moon goddess:

    Selene, Selene, show me in dreams
    What your eyes see, Selene, Selene.

Selene will appear and take you on a journey. Make note of all you see and learn in your *Book of Shadows*, if you have one, or your journal.

HOW TO MAKE MOON WATER

To make moon water, leave a bowl of spring water under the light of the waxing moon for the three nights preceding the full moon. Don't let the sun's direct rays fall upon the bowl.

HERBS, FLOWERS AND VEGETABLES SACRED TO THE MOON

The following plants are aligned to the moon and can nurture your intuition:

- Herbs: clary sage, coriander, ginger, star anise
- Flowers: gardenia, geranium, iris, jasmine, poppy, white rose
- Vegetables: cabbage, cucumber, pumpkin

FULL MOON RITUAL

YOU WILL NEED

- Beautiful white flower (gardenia is perfect)
- Crystal or glass bowl
- Spring water

1. Put the flower in the bowl and fill with spring water. Place the bowl somewhere the moon's rays can fall on it and recite this devotion as you gaze at the moon to honour the goddess:

   Goddess Selene, radiant mistress of the night sky, your silver light dances across the heavens, guiding us through the shadows. You are the essence of mystery and the whisperer of secrets; to gaze upon you is to feel your embrace. Your power flows through us like the tides, stirring the depths of our souls. From your glow wisdom unfolds, and to your celestial realm we shall always wish to return.

   In your honour, may we find joy and strength; may our acts of magick and passion be testament to your grace. Let us embody beauty and resilience, and wield power with compassion, honour with humility and laughter with reverence.

   For we walk the path of the witch, and guided by your light we know the journey is not from without but within. Great Mother, our silent loving companion from the dawn of our existence, in your presence we discover the end of all longing.

2. After you finish meditating on the moon, leave the flower floating in its light. The next day, wear the flower in your hair or pinned to your clothes for luck. You can also dry it as a charm to leave on your altar or use the dried petals in love spells and blessings.

THE SABBATS

When I started practising witchcraft more than 30 years ago, there weren't many books on witchcraft, nor was there social media or the internet. The rare books I could find had always been written in the northern hemisphere. They said I should celebrate Yule (the ongest night) on the winter solstice, between 21 and 23 December. Down under, that's summertime and the summer solstice! It seemed pretty obvious the sabbats were seasonal and needed to be reversed, so when I wrote my first book - *Witch: A Personal Journey* (Random House) - in 1997 I included the sabbats as they corresponded to the southern hemisphere. Nowadays it's easier to understand how the sabbats work. Millions of Instagram posts and TikTok videos explain it as do thousands of books. Even *The Wall Street Journal* says witchcraft is a multi-billion-dollar industry.

So it's probably not necessary but for your convenience here is the Wheel of the Year with our greater and lesser sabbats listed:

SABBAT	SOUTHERN HEMISPHERE	NORTHERN HEMISPHERE
Samhain	1 May	31 October
Yule (depending on the actual solstice)	20-23 June	20-23 December
Imbolc/Candlemas	1 August	2 February
Ostara (depending on the actual equinox)	20-23 September	20-23 March
Beltane	31 October	1 May
Litha (depending on the actual solstice)	20-23 December	20-23 June
Lammas	2 February	1 August
Mabon (depending on the actual equinox)	20-23 March	20-23 September

SABBAT CELEBRATIONS

Here are some ideas to help you celebrate the sabbats. Remember to be reverent and have fun - all acts of love and pleasure are sacred to the Goddess.

Samhain

- Create an ancestor altar with photos, personal and cultural mementos, and offerings of their favourite foods.
- Hold a dumb (silent) supper in honour of deceased loved ones, sharing memories and stories.

Yule

- Light candles or a Yule log, a piece of wood (often oak or pine) decorated with seasonal greenery, candles and symbols to symbolise the return of the sun.
- Decorate an evergreen tree with symbols of protection and renewal.

Imbolc

- Light white candles and set out milk and honey as offerings for the sweetness of life.
- Craft Brigid's crosses of protection (weave straw together to create crosses with equal-sized arms) and conduct a purification ritual to welcome spring.

Ostara (spring equinox)

- Plant seeds or start a garden to symbolise new growth in all areas of your life.
- Decorate eggs and host an egg hunt to honour fertility and rebirth.

Beltane

- Dance around a Maypole and jump over bonfires full of lavender stalks for fertility and purification.
- It's the perfect time to tie the knot! Participate in handfasting ceremonies - either yours or others'! Traditionally, a couple's hands were bound together with ribbon or cord to symbolise their union.

Litha

- Host a bonfire gathering with music, dance and feasting.
- Offer herbs and flowers to the sun by weaving a crown and placing it on your head.

Lammas or Lughnasadh

- Bake organic bread from scratch and share it with loved ones.
- Host a feast using seasonal produce and perform rituals of gratitude for abundance.

Mabon

- Create a harvest altar with fruits, vegetables and grains.
- Reflect on personal balance and acknowledge the fruits of your labour using meditation and journaling.

CRYSTALS

Witches believe nature is sacred. All things in the natural world have a magickal power that we can directly experience because we too are born of this natural world. Crystals are packed with 'earth' power - they are born of the earth and most 'grow' within it until they are disturbed or moved by a collector. Witches believe various crystals are aligned to certain qualities and actions, which can be called upon according to the witch's will. We wear them in ceremonial jewellery, use them for healings by placing them on the body, and store them with our herbs and other objects for rituals and spellcasting.

In spellcasting, you can charge your crystals (hold them in your hand and project your energy into them) with your intent to bless the spell and make it more effective.

Note: ensure your crystals are sustainably sourced. When you purchase crystals from a store ask them where they get their supplies from. Do they only purchase ethically and sustainably sourced crystals? Do not buy crystals that are products of destructive practices like fracking and mining.

TOP 5 CRYSTALS FOR THE WITCH

CRYSTAL	POWER	HOW TO USE
1. Amethyst	Psychic power	A member of the quartz family, amethyst is the ultimate psychic stimulator. I always keep some on my altar. It brings peace of mind and can increase beauty and keep love alive. Place amethyst over your third eye when meditating - it assists in connecting you with the universal soul.
2. Clear quartz	Multi-purpose	Clear quartz can take the place of any crystal if you charge it with your intent. The best crystal balls are made of clear quartz. It has piezoelectric qualities, which means it can convert physical energy into electrical energy and vice versa. Keep your quartz out of direct sunlight when using it magickally. Smoky quartz is aligned to men, much like moonstone is aligned to women.
3. Bloodstone	Strength and bravery	Wearing bloodstone encourages fame and recognition for your efforts. It also supports a long life. Soldiers and warriors have worn bloodstone as a talisman. Expectant mothers can wear bloodstone on their left arm until labour to help prevent a miscarriage then swap it to their right arm to help ease delivery.
4. Moonstone	Especially good for women	Moonstone strengthens the will, calms the mind, brings a sense of inner security and encourages happiness - great for those PMT blues! Priestesses wear moonstone as their sacred stone because it changes tint as it becomes attuned to the wearer's energy.
5. Turquoise	Protection and healing	In many Native American cultures, turquoise is thought to protect against snakebites and give the wearer the ability to stand among wild animals without being harmed. It is a powerful healing stone, which you can carry in an amulet bag, wear as jewellery or place on the chakra points to clear negative energy.

TIPS ON CLEANSING CRYSTALS

- Fill a glass or crystal bowl with spring water, place crystals in it and leave outside for a night under the light of a full moon.
- Bury them overnight in the earth, preferably under a healthy tree or plant.
- Wash them in equal parts vinegar and water then polish with a soft cloth.
- Place smaller crystals on a large amethyst cluster to cleanse and empower them.

Note: if you have a crystal ball, don't expose it to sunlight (keep it wrapped in a dark cloth). Any crystals used in divination should only be exposed to moonlight, not sunlight.

PERSONALISED CRYSTAL CLEANER

Attune your crystals to your personal energy by creating this personalised cleanser.

YOU WILL NEED

- 20 ml white vinegar
- 20 ml spring water
- 2 drops frankincense oil
- 1 drop your blood
- Glass bowl
- Dropper bottle

Mix all the ingredients in the glass bowl. Transfer to the dropper bottle then store in the fridge. Add a few drops to the water you cleanse your crystals in.

STUDYING HERBAL LORE

It is worth studying the medicinal use of herbs when learning about their magickal use because the magickal and medicinal qualities of herbs often align. Enquire about a herbal medicine course at your nearest naturopathy college or do one online.

I could recommend many books on herbalism, both magickal and medicinal, but here are a couple of my favourites:

- *Cunningham's Encyclopedia of Magickal Herbs* by Scott Cunningham
- *The Folk-lore of Plants* by Thomas Thiselton-Dyer
- *Master Book of Herbalism* by Paul Beyerl

MAGICKAL HERBS

PARSLEY	To encourage good luck, pull up some parsley root and give as a gift to a friend.
ROSEMARY	Linked with the matriarch of the family, the name rosemary means 'dew of the sea' and it represents fidelity and remembrance. Give a gift of rosemary sprigs to newlyweds. If they each dip a sprig in the wine they toast their union with at their wedding reception, love will always flourish between them.
VERVAIN	Vervain blesses your home with protective and purifying properties. Burn dried vervain leaves as incense, sprinkle vervain-infused water around the home or place sachets of dried vervain in different rooms.
IVY	If ivy grows up a wall it gives protection from malice and misadventure. Wear a garland of ivy around your head to prevent hair loss.
MYRTLE	Only a woman should plant myrtle. Once planted, she should stand over it, spread her skirts around it with dignity and look 'right proud' - the plant will receive the blessings of the goddess.

MAGICKAL KITCHEN

These everyday items are found in most kitchens but also have magickal properties.

Camphor

We put camphor in cupboards and drawers to keep away moths, but it is magickal too. It is a wonderful cleansing herb to rid spaces of negative, unwanted and unhappy energies. With the windows closed, burn some camphor on a charcoal disc in each room. When it has burned, open the windows to allow the smoke to escape, taking the negativity with it.

You can also burn camphor when you're doing tarot reading or other forms of divination. Camphor can help in achieving prophetic dreams. Put a few drops of camphor essential oil on a hankie and place next to your pillow before sleep.

Cedar

Not only good for keeping clothes and objects fresh while in storage, cedar can be burned as incense in a house where a newborn sleeps to bless the baby and bestow good fortune upon them. You can purposefully breathe in the smoke to create a profound and prophetic inner state or consciousness. And you can keep a small piece of cedar in your wallet to 'keep the moths away' and attract money.

Potato

It is a vegetable - but so much more! You can store a potato for a long time, yet when you cut it into pieces it can regenerate into a new plant. In the old days when people lived close to the land, during the last potato harvest of the season, the person who dug up the final potato was called the 'old potato woman' and was considered lucky.

In Peru, the goddess of the potato is Axomamma, the potato mother. Next time you are cutting up a potato, give thanks to Axomamma and ask for her blessings of sustenance for another year.

Rice

If you want rice to grow well, as the women in Sumatra do, let your hair hang loose down your back as you plant it. It will grow thick and well! Most of you won't be growing rice but you can honour the custom by eating rice with your hair hanging loose and offering a portion to the goddess. If you are working with a group (i.e. a coven), share rice together to affirm your magickal bond.

Rice represents fruitfulness, fertility and prosperity, which is why it was traditional to shower newlyweds with it.

ZODIAC HERBS

The following herbs can enhance the positive aspects of your zodiac archetype. Consume them in food, drink them as teas, wear them as essential oils or use them in an oil burner.

ZODIAC ARCHETYPE	DESCRIPTION	HERBS
Aries	You are fiery and independent.	Chilli, marjoram
Taurus	A seeker of stability, you appreciate the finer things in life.	Cumin, apple blossom
Gemini	Known for their ability to see both sides of the coin, you are a good speaker but can be easily distracted.	Dill, horehound
Cancer	You are the most sensitive and vulnerable, but also the most giving and caring of the zodiac.	St Mary's thistle, hyssop, jasmine
Leo	You're a natural entertainer who loves pleasing others, but watch out you don't become dependent on others' approval.	Bay laurel, sage

ZODIAC ARCHETYPE	DESCRIPTION	HERBS
Virgo	While you can be orderly and sometimes picky, you are very clear on what you want.	Lavender, verbena
Libra	Balanced and able to weigh up all options, you thrive in the company of others.	Bergamot, rose geranium
Scorpio	The most intense of the zodiac archetypes, you are capable of being a celibate hermit one minute and a lusty animal the next!	Basil, guarana, patchouli
Sagittarius	As a seeker of constant challenge, you can sometimes be overly competitive.	Dandelion, echinacea
Capricorn	You are good at setting and achieving long-term goals - sometimes to the exclusion of others' needs.	Rosemary, comfrey
Aquarius	Very curious and capable of child-like wonder in everyday things, you have great social skills but can be forgetful.	Star anise, valerian
Pisces	You are intuitive, visionary and artistic, but can be prone to insecurity and paranoia.	Passionflower, seaweed

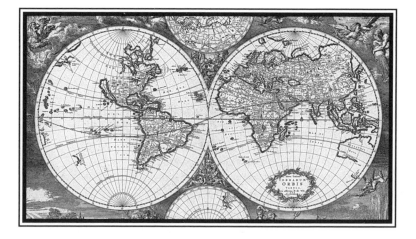

COLOUR BREATHING

Breathe in colours to heal and inspire yourself. Breathing in colours has a positive impact on your well-being, invigorating your senses and uplifting your mood. Begin each colour breathing session with a moment of quiet reflection, grounding yourself in the present moment. Then take a deep breath and imagine inhaling the vibrant energy of the colour that best aligns with your needs.

COLOUR	SYMBOLISM	DESCRIPTION
Gold	Sunshine	Gold infuses you with warmth and positivity, energising your spirit and brightening your outlook.
Azure blue	Clear skies	Azure calms your mind and soothes your soul, bringing a sense of peace and tranquillity.
Rich red	Flames	Red ignites your passion, creativity and imagination, and sparks inspiration.
Verdant green	Lush grass	Green promotes growth and renewal, revitalising your energy and fostering a sense of abundance.
Soft pink	A baby's cheeks	Pink cultivates love and compassion, opening your heart to kindness and connection.
Rich indigo	Centre of a violet	Indigo expands your awareness and intuition, encouraging introspection and deep inner wisdom.

After each breath, savour the sensation and reflect on the qualities of the colour you've just experienced. Let yourself fully embody its essence before moving to the next hue. With each breath, you're nourishing your spirit and embracing the magic of colour in your life.

WITCHY YOGA OF THE BREATH

You can expand this concept into chakra colour breathing. Study the following chart then breathe each colour into the corresponding chakra area. As you do this, see the colour spinning like a wheel. This activates the chakras, clears any trapped energy and helps their optimal functioning.

COLOUR	CHAKRA	DESCRIPTION
Red	Muladhara (root chakra)	Red is associated with the root chakra, which governs our sense of safety, security and stability. It represents our connection to the earth, survival instincts and ability to feel grounded and rooted in the present moment.
Orange	Svadhisthana (sacral chakra)	Orange corresponds to the sacral chakra, which is linked to our creativity, passion and emotional expression. It relates to experiencing pleasure, joy and sensuality, as well as our capacity for healthy relationships and intimacy.
Yellow	Manipura (solar plexus chakra)	Yellow is connected to the solar plexus chakra, which governs our personal power, self-confidence and sense of identity. It represents our ability to assert ourselves, make decisions and pursue our goals with clarity and determination.
Green	Anahata (heart chakra)	Green is associated with the heart chakra, the centre of love, compassion and emotional balance. It relates to giving and receiving love, experiencing empathy and forgiveness, and cultivating harmonious relationships with others and ourselves.

COLOUR	CHAKRA	DESCRIPTION
Blue	Vishuddha (throat chakra)	Blue corresponds to the throat chakra, which governs communication, self-expression and authenticity. It relates to speaking our truth, expressing our thoughts and feelings, and listening with empathy and understanding.
Indigo	Ajna (third-eye chakra)	Indigo is linked to the third-eye chakra, which is associated with intuition, insight and inner wisdom. It represents trusting our inner guidance, accessing higher knowledge and perceiving the deeper truths that lie beyond the physical realm.
Violet	Sahasrara (crown chakra)	Violet corresponds to the crown chakra, the centre of spirituality, consciousness and enlightenment. It represents our connection to the divine, our sense of oneness with the universe, and our ability to transcend ego and experience higher states of consciousness.

These colours and their corresponding chakras form a holistic system of energy centres within the body, which each contribute to our physical, emotional, mental and spiritual well-being. By understanding and balancing the chakras, we can cultivate greater harmony, vitality and wholeness in our lives.

Breath stimulates *prana*, which is Sanskrit for 'breath or life force'. Prana permeates everything in the universe, including the human body. In yoga, breathwork is known as *pranayama*, meaning 'the controlled intake and outflow of breath', which serves as the conduit through which prana flows within the body. Through conscious breath control and regulation, practitioners aim to manipulate the flow of prana, fostering their physical, mental and spiritual well-being. In this way, breath is a tangible vehicle for accessing and channelling prana, allowing individuals to harness its transformative power for holistic health and inner harmony.

When you work with breath and colour, you are stimulating this vital life force, tapping into the co-creative energies of the universe and enhancing your personal magick. You'll soon find yourself practising witchy yoga of the breath!

MAGICKAL BATH

Baths are made magickal by using certain herbs, scented and coloured candles, and even coloured flowers that correspond with your magickal goal. For extra potency, bathe on the night of the full moon.

TO ATTRACT LOVE	Pink candle, roses or jasmine flowers, and a muslin sachet (or stocking) filled with lemon balm (or scatter the leaves on the water)
TO COMMUNE WITH NATURE	Green candle, vases of beautifully coloured and shaped leaves, and a bunch of parsley hung under the tap so the water runs through it
FOR INSPIRATION	Yellow candle, marigold flowers or red hibiscus, and a sachet of angelica herb
FOR COURAGE	Orange candle, red gerberas and a sachet of borage
TO INCREASE BEAUTY	Violet candle, pansies and a sachet of heather blossoms

BEACH MEDITATION RITUAL

Here's something witchy to do at the beach when you don't feel like reading novels, scrolling on your smartphone, or perving at guys or girls.

You will need
- Seaweed collected from the beach

1. Collect enough seaweed to make a giant pentagram. Place strips of it on the sand to form the witches' sacred five-pointed star. Face the top point towards the ocean to draw on its energy. Seaweed is blessed by mother ocean so it will enhance your meditation.

2. Sit in the centre of the pentagram, close your eyes and breathe deeply. Don't try to focus on a particular thing, allow your thoughts to drift in and out of your consciousness. If you like you can chant a mantra of your creation over and over, or perhaps use the following lyrics from a song I performed with my '90s band, Def FX. The song is called 'Under the Blue' and the lyrics are drawn from a ritual I created.

   Mother ocean all around me
   Wrap yourself around my soul
   Flow into my imagination
   A mirror of the whole

3. Repeat this to yourself either silently or aloud until you are completely receptive to the energy of mother ocean. Take note of any visions or thoughts that come to you - these will help guide you through the coming year.

4. Trace words that represent your visions on the water's edge, letting mother ocean flow over them to further bless them and bring them to fruition.

SACRED PICNIC

Choose a location where you can be close to the four elements - air, earth, fire and water - by the ocean or a lake or river. Make sure you can have candles or a fire, and there's privacy so you can go skyclad if you choose.

Prepare simple foods with nourishing and magickal benefits:

- Cornbread with caraway seeds (for good fortune and love)
- Basil pesto (for harmony)
- Fish or tofu seasoned with lemon, parsley, sage and garlic (for wisdom, insight and purity)
- Root vegetable salad (for security and strength)
- Wine or grape juice (for happiness and opulence)
- Apple pie (for love)

During your picnic, read inspirational poetry and stories. Meditate on the wonder of being alive; you can do a tree meditation if you wish.

Find a tree you feel drawn to. Circle it three times sunwise (clockwise in the northern hemisphere, anticlockwise in the southern hemisphere) then sit leaning your back against it. Close your eyes and open your mind to the tree's energy. Be aware of sensations and visions, and be prepared to learn something as the tree imparts its wisdom. When you are ready, kiss the trunk of the tree in thanks and continue with your picnic.

You can do any spellcasting you may desire to do. Remember to pour some wine or grape juice on the earth as a libation for the goddess and leave a food offering for the god.

Leave with everything you arrived with so not a trace of you remains, except perhaps a lock of your hair tied to the tree as an offering, or the initials of everyone at the picnic traced in the earth.

TAROT-READING ASSISTANCE

To assist in reading the cards:

1. Light four white candles and drink mugwort tea.

2. Burn myrrh, sandalwood and cinnamon incense.

3. Say a prayer or statement of intention before shuffling the cards: 'May I be of service to the person I am reading for and help guide them in a useful and constructive way.'

4. Place a chrysolite crystal with the cards or wear it during a reading to assist in a clear reading.

The best advice I can give after reading tarot for 30 years is to trust your first thought and don't second-guess. The first thing coming into your mind as you interpret the cards is always the clearest thought. You can elaborate and expand on this, of course, but trust your gut and the first thought.

MOJO BAGS

Use mojo bags to imbue your life with their magickal powers as you carry them with you. To personalise a mojo bag, add a personal relic to the bag - perhaps some of your hair or nail clippings or an object with great personal meaning. Alternatively, you can kiss the bag three times to align it with your intention and energy.

NAME	PURPOSE	YOU WILL NEED
The Austin Powers mojo bag	To rev up your sex drive ... oh be-*have*!	Red bag 7 apple seeds 7 pinches orris root powder A few drops patchouli oil (for boys) or rose geranium oil (for girls)
Money mojo	To bring money to you	Green bag 1 hair of a black cat (or a piece of black obsidian crystal) A few drops pennyroyal oil (use mint if you are pregnant)
Car mojo	To protect against thieves, mechanical faults and parking tickets	White bag 3 cat claws 3 whiskers A few drops lemon oil
Altar mojo	For a more powerful working space that lets you thrive in your job	Blue bag 1 dried lizard A few drops petitgrain oil
Jury mojo	For success and favour with the judge and jury	Yellow bag Piece of galangal root Ashes of High John the Conqueror root A few drops olive oil
Gambling mojo	To encourage good fortune	Orange bag 1 nutmeg kernel 1 piece silver A few drops orange oil
Home mojo	For a happy home (hang over your kitchen door)	Blue bag 1 star anise A few drops cinnamon oil
The getting of wisdom mojo	To gain insight and make wise choices	Purple bag 1 snake skin 1 amethyst A few drops violet oil

PROTECTION MOJO BAG

Use this bag to protect yourself from jinxes caused by walking under ladders and similar. Make this bag as the moon waxes on a Saturday.

You will need

- Piece of High John the Conqueror root
- Piece of agate
- 3 pinches St John's wort
- 1 red mojo bag (small drawstring bag of natural fabric)
- Olive oil

Place the root, agate and St John's wort in the bag, then seal and cross the bag with your index finger dipped in some olive oil. Carry this bag for protection. Every Saturday, cross it again with the oil to re-empower it.

JINX-REMOVING OIL

In a small bottle, blend 3 drops bergamot essential oil and 2 drops lemon oil. Top with olive oil.

PROTECTION RITUAL

Sometimes you know people who need help - they may be refugees, victims of crime or friends who have hit hard times. This is a simple ritual of love and protection for them.

You will need

- Photo of the person needing protection
- Purple or white candle
- Essential oils such as aloe, borage, clary, cumin, fennel, frankincense, horehound, juniper, rosemary, rue, star anise, thyme and vervain

1. Make an altar that features the photo of the person or people who need protection.

2. Anoint the candle for protection and energy assistance with a blend of at least three herbal oils. If you don't have the extracted herbal oils, infuse some of the fresh herb in olive oil for at least a week in a dark place. Strain before using.

3. Light the candle, gaze at the photo, and ask the goddess to help and bless those you feel need assistance and protection.

HEXES

Here are some light-hearted hexes.

Hex for someone who takes your parking space

This is when someone regularly parks in your spot at work or at your apartment block, or in front of your house. Gather a small item belonging to the person who took your parking space, such as a piece of paper with their name or a belonging of theirs. Place it in a jar or container.

Holding the jar, chant this charm:

In the realm of asphalt and lines,
Your trespass steals what's rightfully mine.
Find another, make it right,
Or face the curse, in parking plight.

Place the jar in a visible spot near your parking space, envisioning the inconvenience the person has caused you being reflected back to them until they never park in your space again.

Hex for someone who cuts you off on the road

Write down the car's number plate or the make and colour (if you didn't see the number plate) on a small piece of paper. Fold over the paper three times as you chant this charm:

> By the roads we all must share,
> Your reckless act, I cannot bear.
> Feel the consequences, swift and true,
> Until you learn, the hex ensues.

Bury or place the paper at the side of the road where the person cut you off. Visualise the person experiencing inconveniences or setbacks in their travels until they learn to drive with more consideration. This spell can influence all drivers in the area to drive more carefully.

Alternatively, you can say this quick hex charm as you are driving:

> Cut me off! Now here's a jinx,
> May your car break down and your luck stink.
> May honking cars follow where you steer,
> Until you learn driving manners, my dear!

Note: as a responsible witch, I must stress the importance of promoting safety and kindness on the road. Instead of resorting to hexes or negative energy, consider using a positive affirmation or mantra to help calm yourself and promote safe driving practices. For example, you might say to yourself: 'I choose to drive safely and remain calm, regardless of others' actions on the road.' This can help you maintain focus and composure, reducing the likelihood of you engaging in road rage or retaliatory behaviour. Also keep some rose quartz mala beads to thumb when you're sitting in traffic to encourage loving calm energy. And hang an evil eye charm from your rear-vision mirror to keep those annoying, dangerous drivers away from you!

Hex for getting rid of sloppy drunks

If someone is bothering you at a bar, see if you can reach their glass. Pour a little of their drink on the floor as you mutter this charm under your breath:

As the spirits blur your sight,
Time to bid this scene goodnight!
With this charm, may you find the door
Sober up and bother me no more!

Then give the person the evil eye ... they'll stumble away and bother you no more. If you can't get to their drink - pour a little of your own on the ground at their feet.

HOW TO DISMANTLE A SPELL SOMEONE ELSE HAS PLACED ON YOU

You WILL NEED

- White sage smudge stick
- Garlic clove necklace
- Thick red cord to tie around your waist

1. Purify yourself by burning the smudge stick and walking through the smoke three times. Place the necklace of garlic around your neck and wrap the red cord around your waist.

2. Tie knots in one end of the cord as you say the following incantation:

By one, this unhexing work's begun.
By two, from me flows the spell impure.
By three, the final hold is free.
By four, I am bewitched no more.

3. Tie one more knot in the cord and say: 'So mote it be.' The knots have drawn the spell out of you and sealed them in the cord. Pull the cord from your waist and bury it somewhere far away (if possible, in the backyard of the person who bewitched you to give the spell back to them).

Note: you can also carry a sprig of angelica with you to ward off further enchantments.

TO REVERSE A CURSE

You will need
- Salt
- Rue herb
- Black candle
- Knife, for carving
- Candle holder

1. Make a circle of salt and rue.
2. Into the black candle, carve your name with the knife then lick your thumb and trace over the carving with your saliva.
3. Expose the wick at the bottom of the candle using the knife, then stand the candle upside down in the candle holder and light the exposed wick. As it burns say:

   I reverse the blight upon me.
   All power is now mine.
   I free myself from the bondage of hatred.
   The curse is lifted – my life is sacred.

Keep the candle burning upside down until there is no more - the curse will be lifted.

TO BREAK A BINDING SPELL

You will need

- Piece of black cloth
- Scissors
- Piece of paper
- Red ink, and pen or quill
- Patchouli essential oil
- 1 black candle
- High John the Conqueror root or frankincense incense
- Charcoal disc
- Bible

1. On a Saturday night during the waning moon, create a poppet (a small doll of white cloth stuffed with cotton or similar) using black cloth and scissors. Assign it the name of the individual who has ensnared you. On the piece of paper, write their name in red ink and affix it to the poppet. Apply the patchouli oil to the poppet and light a black candle. Burn High John the Conqueror root or frankincense incense on a charcoal disc as you hold the poppet, stating this charm:

   Malevolent force, your harm I defy,
   With this spell, your evil shall die.
   Your influence, now firmly barred,
   My power reigns, strong and unmarred.
   Divine justice, by my side,
   Your defeat, forever, I abide.
   Ominous one, your schemes undone,
   Against me your malice will succumb.
   With harm to none, my will shall be,
   So mote it be, is my decree.

2. Snip off a piece of the poppet and repeat the charm twice more, snipping off another piece each time. Read Psalm 7 from the

Bible three times as the incense burns. Let the candle burn for an hour then snuff.

3. Repeat this process every night until there's no more poppet left to snip. Bury the poppet pieces, incense dust and drip the final wax of the candle onto the earth as you read Psalm 7 over the spot.

FOR NAUGHTY WITCHES WHO HAVE BEEN DOING TOO MUCH HEXING

You will need
- Parchment or paper
- Black pen or ink
- Clean pin
- Gold candle (for the blessings of Sol, the Roman sun god)
- Frankincense incense
- Myrrh incense
- Charcoal disc
- Brass dish
- Soap and water

1. On a Sunday morning as the sun rises, write a list of all the bad things you've done on the parchment in black ink. Then prick your thumb with the pin and press a thumbprint of your blood on the parchment.

2. Light the candle. Burn the frankincense and myrrh on the charcoal disc in the dish as you read your list and feel truly remorseful. When you feel ready, light the list in the candle's flame and throw it into the dish to burn.

3. When everything has burned and only ashes remain, rub your hands with these ashes then wash your hands with soap and water as you say:

> *My past is cleansed, my future bright,*
> *With humble heart, I set things right.*
> *Undo the wrongs, work for the best,*
> *I conjure peace – no more unrest.*

4. Dry your hands in the warmth of the candle flame and sun. You now have a clean magickal slate!

HEALTH AND PHYSICAL WELL-BEING

COLD AND FLU CHARM AWAY

You will need

- Enough blue cord to wrap around your wrist or ankle thrice (three times)
- Eucalyptus or tea tree essential oil

1. Tie a knot in the cord, dab it with some oil and say: 'Cold be gone, body be strong.'
2. Tie another knot further along the cord, dab with oil and say again: 'Cold be gone, body be strong.' Repeat this process three more times (for a total of five knots) then tie the cord around your wrist or ankle as you say: 'So mote it be.'
3. Wear the cord for 24 hours and your symptoms should abate. Go to the doctor or naturopath if they don't!

STRENGTHEN KIDDIES' IMMUNE SYSTEMS

You will need

- Echinacea
- Mint
- Honey
- Knife, for carving
- Blue candle

1. Every morning before school, prepare a tea with the echinacea and mint then sweeten with a little honey.
2. Gather the kids around the kitchen table and carve each of their initials into the blue candle (for health). Light the candle and say together:

Our magick tea makes us strong.
We are healthy and happy all day long.

3. All sip the tea together (make sure it's lukewarm not boiling; it's important to drink the tea easily and energetically). Reinforce your children's confidence and happiness by complimenting them on what special gorgeous creatures they are before they head off to school. (Happiness and confidence are huge immune-system boosters.) Also make sure they're taking vitamin C. They should sail through school without picking up all the bugs!

ITCHY PALMS

Itchy palms mean money is coming ... but you could have a weak liver. Drink dandelion root tea and take St Mary's thistle pills (available from health-food stores).

SPELL FOR A SORE BACK

Have a warm bath with a cup of chamomile infusion poured in. Drink a cup of chamomile tea as well. For added effectiveness, break 3 bay leaves off a living branch to add to the bath - make sure you break them in a 'downward' motion to assist in their 'purging pain' properties.

WILLOW PAIN RELEASE

Stand beside a flowing river or stream with a leafy willow branch in your right hand. Stroke your back with the branch as you say: 'Away, away with pain.' Repeat at least three times, then throw the branch into the river to carry the pain away.

MAGICKAL RELIEF OF MIGRAINES

First, if you are suffering frequent migraines, get thee to the doctor! Also try these remedies:

- Drink lavender tea. (Place a small handful of dried lavender in a pot of nearly boiling water and steep for 5 minutes.) Queen Elizabeth I drank 10 cups of lavender tea a day to ease her brain strain.
- For additional help, add a few sprigs of rosemary to lavender tea; it is a soothing brain tonic.
- Try a cool compress over the eyes. Add a few drops lavender oil to the compress to help ease the pain.

INDIGENOUS AUSTRALIAN HEADACHE CURE

Have a trusted loved one who is healthy and never gets headaches to sit cross-legged beside you. Place one end of a long piece of red string in your mouth and the other end in the other person's mouth. The other person then draws the string through their mouth away from you so they 'draw' the headache out. When the string has finished moving from your mouth through theirs, they need to spit and bury the string.

TO RELEASE MIGRAINE-CAUSING CONTROL ISSUES

Sometimes chronic migraines can be caused by you having control issues in your life - trying to control others and yourself to the point of stifling your natural energy. Try wearing a sapphire ring on the index finger of your right hand to help channel this energy into more constructive avenues.

PAIN POTION

For chronic pain, see your doctor or naturopath - but this will help in the meantime! Make this potion on a full moon.

You WILL NEED

- Willow bark tea (available from health-food shops)
- 1 litre spring water
- Dash of sugar syrup
- Glass bottle or container
- 1 blue lace agate crystal

1. Brew a strong willow bark tea with the spring water (don't boil just simmer in a saucepan) and stir in a little sugar syrup. Place in a glass bottle with the blue lace agate.

2. Stand under the full moon holding up the potion for blessing as you say:

   Lady of Night, heed my plight.
   I charge this potion with your light.
   Now sacred liquid you shall be
   Enchanted to make me pain-free.

3. Kiss the bottle three times. Then keep in the fridge and drink ½ cup of potion every morning. No one else should drink this potion; it is enchanted to be aligned with you.

HEALING THOUGHTS
FOR ARTHRITIS

If you or anyone you know has skin or arthritis problems, a cup of aloe vera juice in their bathwater and a capful taken internally is helpful.

Celery seed extract is also excellent for arthritis. Make an enchanted tea from it by placing 1 teaspoon celery seeds in hot water. Stir sunwise (clockwise in the northern hemisphere, anticlockwise in the southern hemisphere) as you say this charm:

> *Arthritis's grip, I bid to fade,*
> *Like morning mist at light of dawn,*
> *Restore the joints, release the pain.*
> *Now strength and life reborn.*

HEALING SPELL AFTER SURGERY

You will need

- 3 drops lavender essential oil
- 3 drops sandalwood essential oil
- Knife, for carving
- 1 blue candle

1. Mix the oils together to create a healing blend. Carve your name in the blue candle. Lick your thumb and trace over your name with saliva then anoint that with healing oil.

2. Burn the candle for an hour a day. At least three times, place your right hand above the flame and absorb its healing heat as you say:

   Power of fire,
   Warm me well.
   Heal this body
   In which I dwell.

3. Do this every day, getting a new candle and mixing new oil when necessary until you are completely healed.

   Note: the incantation refers to you 'dwelling' in this body. This is to remind you that you are not this sickness or injury. You are an infinite light being. You can align your spiritual self with the healing energy of fire and supercharge your body's recovery.

GROWING AND HEALING

Grow a pot of sage and rue from seedlings. Nurture them; as they grow together, so will you heal faster without future complications.

MALE PARTNER HEALING SPELL

Do this for a male partner or friend who is suffering.

You WILL NEED

- 3 drops patchouli essential oil
- 3 drops cypress essential oil
- 1 teaspoon jojoba oil
- Myrrh incense
- Cinnamon incense

1. Mix the oils together and massage into the soles of your partner or friend's feet - it will help him walk strong.
2. Burn incense of myrrh and cinnamon (buy individual sticks or blend them yourself and burn on charcoal discs). Have him walk through the smoke three times or fan the smoke over him as you do three revolutions of his body.

FEMALE PARTNER HEALING SPELL

You WILL NEED

- Knife, for carving
- 1 pink candle
- Lavender and chamomile flowers (dried or fresh)
- Neroli essential oil

1. Carve your partner or friend's name into the candle and surround it with a wreath of flowers. With your index finger, paint over her name with the neroli oil. Focus on your desire to see her happy and healed.
2. Light the candle and say:

> *Great goddess of the moon*
> *Maiden mother crone.*

Heal the woman I love
Free her from her woe.
Hold her fast in love and light
So that she may rise from this long night
This I ask for the good of all
So mote it be.

3. Take the flowers outside and place at the base of a tree or plant as an offering to the goddess. Thank her for her help.

HELP FOR STOPPING SMOKING

Flush away addiction spell

Every morning before you go to the loo, drink 1 cup liquorice tea. When you go to the loo imagine your addiction draining away from you. As you flush say:
Flush away,
Flush away.
Banned by night,
Gone by day.
Repeat this charm three times as the water and your addiction gurgle away.

Wean off smoking cigarettes

Here is a British herb tobacco mixture that you might like to smoke in rolling papers instead of cigarettes to help wean you off nicotine. Mix equal quantities of coltsfoot, buckbean, eyebright, betony, rosemary, thyme, lavender and chamomile. This is also a good remedy for asthma and bronchial congestion.

HELP TO STOP SNORING

Some practical tips: sleep on your side and don't drink alcohol before bed.

You will need
- Piece of white paper
- Graphite pencil
- Eraser

Write 'I snore' on the paper in pencil then rub it out with the eraser. Write and rub it out again seven times. Sleep with the paper under your pillow. Use a new piece every night until the problem stops.

WITCH'S RECIPE FOR REMOVING FRECKLES

You will need
- 1 handful fresh yarrow leaves, chopped
- 1 horseradish root, grated
- 1 litre filtered water

1. Mix the yarrow and horseradish in a pot of water. Bring to the boil, simmering for 20 minutes until it reduces. Strain and cool.
2. Keep in a dark place and apply to your freckles each morning and night. As you do this say:

   Freckles, freckles go away.
   clear skin now is mine to stay.

WITCH BREATH

Here's a witchy dental gargle you can make to clean the mouth and numb it if there is pain. Mix 2 drops clove essential oil in ½ cup warm spring water with ½ teaspoon salt. Gargle well, swishing around the mouth - the salt will clean and cloves will numb. Humbly ask for the pain-relieving blessings of the coca gods while you're at it!

DENTAL DRAMAS

If you're finding yourself in an endless cycle of dental dramas, having repeated dental work and constantly suffering with oral discomfort, consider doing the following:

In South America, coca leaves mixed with cocaine is considered a sacred funeral herb. Some people will bury parcels of coca leaves with their dead loved ones. They believe this will please the spirits and make entry to the next world easier.

In the western world, coca leaves are unavailable so it's unlikely anyone would bury coca. If you want to ask for the blessings of the gods while having dental work, the next time you have an injection of novocaine (which is made from coca), think of that injection as being pleasing to the coca gods. They can release you from pain and stop it from returning.

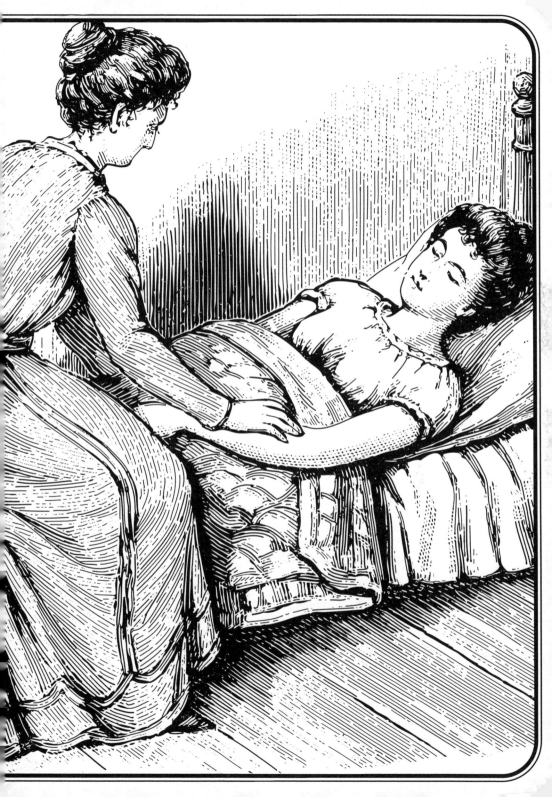

SELF-IMAGE
AND MENTAL
WELL-BEING

ADVICE TO EASE DEPRESSION

Try an aromatherapy oil blend based on clary sage (note that it's contraindicated in pregnancy). There are so many amazing brands and blends of oils now, but when I first got into using oils in the 1980s, there was hardly anything! I loved the Wise Women blend from Australian brand Jurlique. They don't make that blend anymore - but their Balance blend is exceptional. When I started living a witchy life, Jurlique was a small independent supplier based in Adelaide. They are still the best for oils and skincare. So pure, with everything grown on their farm ... which is a lot larger now!

Their Balance blend has the following oils:

- Australian mandarin
- Geranium
- Lime
- Peru balsam
- Ylang-ylang
- Rose absolute

Try tansy tea

Drink 1 cup tansy tea (this coffee substitute is available at health-food shops). Tansy honours the goddess within and represents the immortal and eternally renewing qualities of life.

St John's wort

Take St John wort's tablets or tincture. Nicolas Culpepper (a renowned herbalist) recommends steeping the herb in wine and drinking a glass before bed to prevent bad dreams. At the time of writing this, I've been sober for nearly 12 years. I like the tea of St John's wort in the evening if I'm feeling mentally challenged. It's very soothing.

SPELL TO EASE DEPRESSION

You will need

- Salt
- 1 stick eucalyptus wood (an excellent conductor)
- 1 white rose

1. Stand under a tree and ask for its help to heal you. Sprinkle a circle of salt at its base. Plunge the stick into the centre of the circle, holding the end in both hands. Channel your feelings of sadness and depression through the stick. If you cry, let your tears fall on the earth as you say:

   I release pain and woe
   From me all sadness flows.
   Heal my heart, Mother Earth
   So I am free of fear and hurt.

2. Take the stick out of the earth. Place the white rose in its place and say:

   I am what I am, and what I am has beauty and strength.

3. Thank the tree and keep the stick to use again if necessary.

A SPELL TO HELP EASE POSTNATAL DEPRESSION

Do this spell on a full moon.

You will need

- 4 drops clary sage essential oil
- Silver bowl
- Spring water
- 1 quartz crystal

1. Anoint yourself with 1 drop clary sage oil over your third eye, 1 drop over your heart and 1 drop in each palm of your hands. Fill the bowl with the spring water.

2. Sit outside under the light of the full moon, holding the quartz crystal in both hands with the water-filled bowl in front of you, charging in the moonlight. Channel your sadness and frustration into the crystal - even say aloud what is depressing you. When you are ready, rinse the crystal through the moon-charged water, washing all the sadness away.

3. Hold the moon-charged quartz to your heart. Looking at the moon, say: 'Mother moon ease my heart, so my life anew can start.'

4. Pour the water at the base of a tree, saying: 'It is done. So mote it be.' Thank the tree for its final neutralising of your sadness. Keep the moon-charged quartz with you.

TO STOP WORRYING

You will need
- 1 white candle
- A few drops vanilla essential oil
- Oil burner
- Small bell or gong

1. Before bed, light the candle and burn the oil in an oil burner. Gaze at the flame, inhale deeply and say three times:
   Sound of harmony,
   Free me of worry.

2. Strike the gong. As the sound fades, so will your worries.

3. Snuff the candle and sleep. Do this every night until your worries are completely gone.

RITUAL FOR EASING ANXIETY ATTACKS

Anxiety attacks can be caused when times of stress have weakened your will and self-determination. Oak tree meditations can restore your faith in your personal vision. The oak is one of the sacred trees of the ancient Celts and Druids.

1. Find an oak tree (perhaps visit your local botanical gardens) and sit with your back against it. Consciously connect with the tree through your heart chakra. Visualise the area over your heart glowing pink or perhaps pale green, and send that light into the tree. Feel it return its essence to you - self-determination, inner strength, courage and endurance. The oak tree can be a doorway to what lies beyond your current situation.

2. Keeping your eyes closed, open your heart and mind to the oak tree's lesson and gift.

3. When you have finished, thank the tree and leave an offering. (Even a kiss on the tree's trunk will be appreciated!) Or better still, make a donation to an environmental conservation group that saves trees.

Try to do this meditation at least twice a week until you feel better. Ideally you'd do it every morning for seven days to ease your problem.

IF YOU FIND YOURSELF DRINKING ALCOHOL WHEN SAD

Wine drinking when you're sad, especially among women, has become commercialised to the point that there are tea-towels proudly proclaiming: 'It's wine o'clock somewhere.' If you find yourself succumbing to this subtle coercion, do the following: place a sprig of rosemary in your glass of wine to limit the wine's 'boozy' depressive effect.

TO STOP LOSING YOUR PATIENCE

YOU WILL NEED

- 1 yellow candle, for intellect and rationality
- Lavender incense, for calm
- Wind-up clock, for conjuring time

1. By the light of the yellow candle, light the incense, then inhale and sit quietly. Slowly wind the clock hands backwards as you intone:
    There is time for everything to be
    In its place and orderly.
    I free my space in good grace,
    Everything has its time and place.

2. Repeat this as you keep winding the clock backwards. Leave the candle and clock by your bed and repeat this ritual every night for seven nights.

A SPELL TIP FOR CLARITY OF THOUGHT

This spell is for when you have a serious problem with constantly being vague.

YOU WILL NEED

- Rosemary seeds or seedlings
- Some pieces of citrine quartz

1. Grow your own rosemary plant, nurturing it from seeds or seedlings. Stud the soil around the base of the plant with citrine quartz. You need to develop a close bond with this plant, which is renowned for its mental enhancing abilities.

2. When the plant is flourishing, cut a little of the leaf and brew some rosemary tea. Drink the tea in the light of the morning sun. As you inhale the steam say this charm:

   Rosemary, dew of the sea, your presence revives me, your scent inspires m3.

3. Drink this tea every morning. Wear some rosemary in your hair or carry some in your pocket. (The ancient Greek scholars used to entwine rosemary in their hair to help memory and logical thought processes.

4. Take one of the pieces of citrine quartz with you throughout the day then replace it in the soil at night to recharge.

FOCUS AND WILLPOWER

To gain keener mental ability and willpower, burn this incense.

You will need

- 1 teaspoon sandalwood
- 2 teaspoons frankincense
- ¼ cup uva ursi leaves (shrub with flowers and red berries)
- 1 teaspoon powdered nutmeg
- 1 teaspoon orris root
- Charcoal disc

1. On a Wednesday as the moon waxes, grind all the ingredients except the charcoal in a mortar and pestle as you say:
   Focus and will
   Shall be mine.
   Holy herbs empower
   Thoughts of mine.
2. Burn the incense regularly on charcoal discs.

5-CANDLE SPELL TO IMPROVE WILLPOWER

Important: make sure your candles are the dripping wax kind!

You will need

- White, blue, green, red and yellow candles

1. Thinking strongly about your goal or desire, light the white candle first then light the others from its flame as you say:
   Candles burning, candles bright,
   My will is strong, success is mine.

2. As the candles burn, collect the soft wax and mould it into balls, carving a special rune or symbol into them. (I use the runic symbol Uruz, which is tattooed on my arm and represents tenacity and strength in adversity).

3. As you carve the symbol, focus strongly on your goal. Each ball of wax holds the essence of your desire - it's like a seal keeping your magickal energies contained and focused on your desire. Place the balls in a sacred space with care. As long as they are there, they'll continue to work the spell for you. All the willpower you need will be yours!

VITALITY RITUALS

Colour breathing

When you are feeling low on energy try colour breathing (see pages 41-42). Taking deep breaths, imagine the air as a stream of silver light as you breathe in, then gold as you breathe out. Feel the light infuse every fibre of your being so you feel tingly and awake.

Ball of light

Another technique is to loosely cup your 'power hand' (the hand you write with) and visualise a ball of light growing there, glowing and pulsing. Throw the ball of light into your mouth and swallow, or throw it into your coffee or herbal tea for extra energy.

Vitality baths

Take regular baths with lots of lavender oil, a handful of sea salt and a piece of smoky quartz sitting on the bottom of the tub to help strip away collected negative energies that can weigh you down.

Sea salt cleansing

Throw a handful of sea salt on the floor of the shower and stand on it while you wash. Visualise any toxic energy being cleared and nullified by the swirling water energy as it goes down the drain.

SPELL FOR HAPPINESS

You will need
- 1 black candle
- Small box (cardboard or wood)
- Piece of linen
- 3 drops lavender essential oil
- Vase of beautiful, coloured flowers
- 1 silver candle
- Mandarin essential oil
- Handful each of vervain and yarrow herbs
- Lock of your hair
- 1 yellow ribbon

1. Set up an altar in your home, such as the top of a small table or chest, where it won't be disturbed. Place the black candle at the back with the box, leaving everything else off the altar for the moment.

2. Light the candle. Sit in front and invoke the ancient Roman goddess Diana, the queen of the witches:

   Diana, queen of the heavens, bless me with your divine presence.

3. Feel her come to you as a serene yet incredibly strong and powerful presence. Now focus on the sadness you wish to release (you are safe in Diana's arms), letting it pour out of you. Catch a tear with the linen, placing it in the box. When you are ready, drop lavender oil on the linen saying:

   I release you, I release you, I release you.

4. Place the lid on the box and snuff the black candle with your fingertips. While it's important to honour and acknowledge your sadness as valid and justified, it's now time to let it go.

5. Place the vase of flowers on the altar with the silver candle, lighting it. Anoint yourself at the heart and third-eye chakras with the mandarin oil. Take the mixture of herbs and sprinkle them in a sunwise (clockwise in the northern hemisphere, anticlockwise in the southern hemisphere) direction to make a circle on your altar. In the centre of the circle, place your lock of hair and the ribbon.

6. Holding your hands over these items, ask Diana to move her energy through you so you can fortify them with the strongest and purest essence of your life force. Feel her love move through you like silver light, pulsing out of the palms of your hands and into the herb circle. When you are ready say: 'Above all things I deserve to be happy,' or something similar in your own words that expresses your desire for happiness.

7. Tie the yellow ribbon around the lock of hair three times saying:

> *Sweet joy is bound to me.*
> *Happiness comes easily.*
> *As the tides of life ebb and flow,*
> *I avoid their undertow.*

8. Tie five knots into the ribbon, saying with each knot:

> *By one, this spell is done.*
> *By two, it will come true.*
> *By three, so mote it be.*
> *By four, for the good of all.*
> *By five, so shall love thrive.*

9. Thank the goddess Diana for assisting your rite and bid her love and farewell. Keep the altar set up for as long as you want, relighting the silver candle to re-empower your ritual whenever you need to. (Keep the flowers fresh too! Or perhaps place

a growing pot of vervain there so its life force can continue to build the strength of your spell.) Whenever you need to, meditate in front of your altar on your divine right to be happy, no matter what trials are placed in your path. The greatest and most honourable people often have had the hardest lessons.

BATH FOR A HAPPIER LIFE

You will need

- 4 cups rock salt
- 1 cup Epsom salt
- A few drops pink food colouring
- 3 drops each ylang-ylang, lavender, orange and bergamot essential oils

1. Combine all the ingredients in a glass container and stir to mix. Bathe with ½ cup of this mixture every night. As you lie in the bath, say this incantation:
   Earth and water I conjure thee,
   To work my will for joy to be.
   Salts of life and holy scent,
   Now my dreams are heaven-sent.

2. Relax and see if you can doze off a little or enter a dreamlike state to see visions of your future happiness and good future.

3. The phrase in your charm 'dreams are heaven-sent' recognises that dreams hold a special or divine significance. The content or messages within your dreams are perceived as gifts from a higher power or spiritual realm. Dreams provide insights, guidance or messages that can offer comfort, inspiration or valuable information from a source beyond the realm of ordinary consciousness. When you take your happiness bath, any dreams you experience afterwards are divine communication and connect you to something beyond the tangible realities of everyday life. They can guide you and inspire you to your greatest happiness.

THANK YOU SPELL FOR ALL THE GOOD THINGS IN LIFE

Try this spell when things are going really well and you want to say thanks to universe!

YOU WILL NEED

- Graphite pencil (optional)
- Sandalwood essential oil
- Orange blossom essential oil

1. Make an offering to the earth by planting a tree and giving money to charity to spread the good vibes. Gift a stranger with a smile and a kind word.

2. Stand somewhere under the open sky - whether in nature or on top of a building. Trace your initials on the ground and stand on them. Use a graphite pencil to write them down if you're standing on a building. It's important to stand on your initials to anchor your gratitude as you become a channel of light to magnify it out into the world.

3. Anoint yourself with a few drops sandalwood and orange blossom essential oils then throw your arms in the air and call out this charm:

Under the sky, with heartfelt grace,
Thank you, universe, for sacred space.
From me love and goodwill flow
For the good of all my gratitude shows.
So mote it be, with heartfelt cheer,
I offer this magick far and near.

4. When you have finished, press your hands into the earth or surface beneath you and ground your energy in love and good grace. Then go and eat a lovely grounding meal, knowing that everything is well in your world.

GRATITUDE BATH FOR GOOD FORTUNE

To continue your good fortune, take a gratitude bath every Sunday.

1. Mix 4 cups pure ground rock salt and 1 cup Epsom salt. Put in a glass container with a few drops orange food colouring and stir to mix together. Add 1 drop jasmine, 2 drops orange and 3 drops sandalwood essential oils.

2. Immerse yourself in the bath for at least 15 minutes. Give thanks and encourage continued good fortune by saying this incantation:

   Earth and water I conjure thee,
   To work my will for continued luck to be.
   Salts of life I mix with holy scent
   So my prayers to the Lady and Lord are sent.

THE LADY AND LORD

In modern witchcraft, the Lady and Lord are symbolic representations of the divine feminine and masculine energies, embodying the dual aspects of the universe. The Lady is often associated with the moon, intuition and nurturing qualities, symbolising the creative and receptive forces of nature. The Lord is linked to the sun, strength and protective attributes, embodying the active and transformative energies of the natural world. Together, they form a balanced and harmonious partnership, reflecting the cyclical nature of life and the interconnectedness of all things in the practice of modern witchcraft.

MOULIN ROUGE GLAMOUR SPELL

For when you need to make a big entrance!

1. For this spell, wear colourful clothes that are flamboyant and luscious! If you can't bear to venture out in anything but black, make sure you wear opulent jewellery - stones of topaz, sapphire and ruby.

2. Stand in the centre of four lit red candles that you have anointed with cinnamon oil. You need to invoke the blessings of the night when glamour and mystery abound.

   Guardians of the night, magnify my light.
   Amplify my presence, a beacon in the night.
   Bewitch those in my sight, my allure shall be
   The spell of pleasure cast on all who follow me.

3. In your mind's eye, see the flames leap up and join above your head, spiralling into the cosmos. Know that you are the centre of all beauty and glamour in the universe.

SPELL FOR CONFIDENCE

You WILL NEED
- Piece of cedar wood about 45 cm (18 inches) long
- Rose geranium essential oil

1. Chip off a little of the wood and put to one side. Place 7 drops rose geranium oil onto the cedar wand. Holding it in your right hand, trace a circle around yourself (or have someone do it for you). Visualise a glowing sphere of light encasing you as you say:
   Circle of cedar, strength aligns,
   Anointed courage shall now fly.
   Power shines bold and bright,
   Blessed in confidence and might.
2. Place 1 drop rose geranium oil on the smaller piece of cedar and carry it with you. Repeat this ritual every morning.

   Tip: drinking black tea with lemon is good for courage. Have a cup before performing this ritual.

A YOUNG GIRL OR WOMAN'S SPELL TO INCREASE CONFIDENCE

Invoke the goddess Venus to increase a female's confidence. Venus helps to invoke the spiritual aspect of the self with confidence and ease.

1. At home, make a little altar to Venus. Place on it the Empress card of the tarot, 1 orange candle, 1 pink candle, a vase with a pink tiger lily or similar feminine flower, a piece of rose quartz and some sandalwood incense.

2. Every morning, light the candles and incense and invoke the goddess:

> *I weave my spell of witchy ways*
> *and call on Venus bold and brave.*
> *I feel her within me on this day*
> *And can be myself, bold and brave.*

3. Snuff the candles and incense, ready for the day. Carry the rose quartz with you during the day. When you get home, place it on your altar as an offering and to say thank you to the goddess for her assistance. Repeat this spell daily as necessary.

SPELL TO ATTRACT GOOD FRIENDS

Do this spell on a Thursday during the waxing moon, at the third hour after sunset.

You will need
- Knife, for carving
- 1 blue candle
- 1 drop cedarwood oil
- 1 pinch nutmeg
- Ace of Cups tarot card or a photo of someone whose qualities you admire

1. Carve the symbol for the planet Jupiter (this looks like the number 4 with the top 45-degree stroke curling back a little) into the candle then rub the oil and nutmeg over it.

2. Light the candle, focus on the card or photo, and intone nine times:

> *True friendship comes to me,*
> *Happily, and easily.*

3. Snuff the candle. Repeat this ritual every night for seven nights until the full moon if possible.

Note: take practical action. Be open to accepting invitations, spending time with new groups of people and trusting that your spell is going to pave the way for harmonious, sincere and interesting friendships.

TO ATTRACT POSITIVE PEOPLE IN YOUR LIFE

This spell helps you feel you are worthy of attention from positive people. Place 7 endive leaves in a flat dish just covered by olive oil. Cover with a piece of cloth and let steep for seven days. Strain and use 1 teaspoon of the infused oil in the bath or dab onto your wrists and temples regularly to harmonise your energy with that of positive people.

SPELL FOR HARMONY (TO STOP FIGHTING WITH A FRIEND)

You will need
- Pink and yellow candles
- Lemon essential oil
- 1 basil leaf
- 3 lemons

1. Anoint the candles with lemon oil then light. Place the basil leaf in your mouth (for ease of communication). Juggle the lemons as you say:
    As I spin this juggling spell
    So our friendship shall be well.

2. When you are juggling the lemons effortlessly, keep going for at least three minutes, repeating the incantation. If you drop them, start again. It's important to remain really focused and realise that you are 'spinning' away the dross that has accumulated around your friendship, paving the way for happier and more harmonious interactions.

3. Keep the lemons and re-juggle them as needed for one week - then bury them. Your problem should be resolved, but you can do the spell again with new lemons and candles if you need.

BAD REPUTATION SPELL

You will need
- White sage bundle
- 1 black pebble
- 1 pot filled with loose earth
- 1 stick
- 1 white pebble

1. Smudge your space with sage smoke to purify.

2. Holding the black pebble in both hands, focus on why you have a bad reputation as you say:

> *My deeds have been wrong*
> *But my resolve is now strong.*
> *My bad reputation is going, going, gone.*

3. Push the stone lightly into the pot of earth, using the stick press down on it as you say 'Going, going, gone' three more times, really focusing on erasing your bad reputation. Leave the stick poking up out of the earth.

4. Now hold the white pebble and say:

I manifest a better life.
I am now seen in a new light.

5. See yourself surrounded by people supporting you and thinking well of you. Place the white pebble on the top of the soil.

6. Each day, use the stick to push the black pebble down further, saying 'Going, going, gone.' Hold the white pebble repeating the previous affirmation.

LETTING GO OF THE PAST

You will need

- Paper
- Black box
- Sea salt
- 9 garlic cloves
- Black ribbon

1. Write on the paper what you need to let go of then put it in the box with the salt and place the garlic over it. Focus on your sadness; if you cry, let your tears fall into the box. When you are ready, put the lid on and wrap the ribbon around it, tying off with nine knots. As you do this say:
   Goodbye, goodbye, to the past that dwells here.

2. Bury the box at least 90 cm (3 feet) under a tree. (First ask for the tree's permission - its life force will transform the negativity in the box so it will never affect you again.) When you are finished, walk away without looking back.

SLEEP
AND
DREAMS

A TALISMAN TO HELP
RESTFUL SLEEP

You will need

- 1 handful dried cowslip
- 1 handful dried hops
- 1 handful dried lavender
- Piece of moonstone
- A few drops blue chamomile essential oil
- Pale blue silk pillow

1. Sew all the ingredients into the pillow and place it among your regular sleeping pillows. Hold it in both hands when you get into bed as you recite this charm:

    Morpheus, god of dreams,
    Bless me as I fall asleep.
    Keep me now within your sight
    Safe in your arms I sleep all night.

2. Place it next to your head and go to sleep. Sweet dreams!

SPELL FOR BETTER SLEEP
AND HAPPIER DAYS

Have zero alcohol after 6 pm. Instead, steep fresh marigold petals in hot water. Strain and add ½ teaspoon honey to encourage pleasant dreams. Read something inspiring just before bed or remember a particularly pleasant event in your life to encourage happy dreams and a peaceful sleep.

AROMATHERAPY SLEEP ESSENTIAL OIL BLEND

This blend combines the calming and soothing properties of lavender and chamomile with the grounding and comforting scent of cedarwood, promoting relaxation and a restful night's sleep. Adjust the proportions according to your personal preference and always perform a patch test before applying any new blend to your skin to make sure you don't have any adverse reactions.

INGREDIENTS

- 5 drops lavender essential oil
- 3 drops chamomile essential oil
- 2 drops cedarwood essential oil
- Carrier oil (such as jojoba, sweet almond or fractionated coconut oil)

1. In a small, dark glass bottle, add the essential oils then fill the rest of the bottle with your chosen carrier oil. Cap the bottle tightly and shake gently to mix the oils thoroughly.

2. Before bedtime, apply a few drops of the blend to your wrists, temples, neck or bottoms of your feet. You can also add a few drops to an oil diffuser in your bedroom.

SALUTE THE SUN

If you are a witch, perform the sacred pentagram salute to the sun on going to bed and waking. Touch the index finger of your right hand to your third eye (between the eyebrows), right nipple, left shoulder, right shoulder, left nipple and third eye. The sacred star will bless and protect you.

PASSION SLEEPING SPELL

This is a spell to bring passion into your love life.

You will need

- Rose petals
- Cinnamon powder
- Sandalwood powder
- Dried patchouli leaves
- Charcoal disc
- Piece of pink paper

Sprinkle the rose petals around your bed for seven nights leading up to the full moon (you need to sleep in it alone). Blend the cinnamon, sandalwood and patchouli into a powder incense and burn 1 teaspoon of the mixture on a charcoal disc as you go to sleep. Write your lover's name on the piece of paper and put it under your pillow. You will dream of your passion being fulfilled and understand the way to make this a reality.

FOR THE RELIEF OF NIGHTMARES

- Push fennel seeds into the keyholes of all the doors of your home to keep out unwanted energies and spirits.
- Hang sprigs of fennel over your bed to clear your space of destructive energies.
- Nicolas Culpepper, the 17th-century herbalist, suggests placing a sprig of thyme under your pillow. You can also burn thyme oil while you sleep and add thyme to your cooking.
- Lightly brush a bundle of sage over the sleeping person to disperse fear and negativity.
- Try eating a ripe banana before bed. (Bananas contain L-tryptophan, which helps you sleep well.)

BAD DREAM SPELL

Here's a way to get rid of recurrent bad dreams.

You will need

- Piece of paper
- 1 black candle
- Damiana herbal tea
- Honey

1. Write a graphic description of your dream on the paper. Try to include everything, even dialogue or colours, making it as close to the actual dream as possible.

2. Using the black candle, burn the paper and bury the ashes in the dirt. As you turn the ashes into the soil, intone:

   I release the past,
   I release my fears.
   The dream is gone,
   No longer near.

3. Try drinking some damiana herbal tea with a little honey before you go to bed to encourage pleasant dreams.

FOR A CHILD'S NIGHT TERRORS

Burn lemon essential oil in a burner to assist in peaceful sleep.

1. Keep your child cool - feeling overheated will aggravate the problem.

2. Make a magickal totem to watch over your child. You can create it together by collecting beautiful things from nature - twigs, leaves, fresh petals and flowers (replace as necessary). Form into the shape of a body (bind with silver thread or cord), using feathers for hair and perhaps a lovely flat shell with a smiling face drawn on it.

3. You and your child can empower this totem by passing it through the smoke of burning sage leaves (diffuse them in a saucepan) as you say (both or just you if they are too young):

   Magick Man [or Lady, depending on what your child wants],
   Watch over me.
   Keep me safe and happy
   While I sleep.

Place the totem next to the bed where the child can see it and know that it's watching over them.

LOVE,
SEX AND
RELATION-
SHIPS

TO MAKE ANOTHER NOTICE YOU

While you can't interfere with another's free will by making them fall in love with you, you *can* do this spell to make them notice you!

You will need

- 1 very red apple
- 1 red pen
- Piece of blue paper
- 2 teaspoons liquid honey
- 3 drops violet essential oil (or neroli but violet's best)
- White ribbon

1. Cut the top off the apple and remove the core, reserving the seeds. With the red pen, write the name of the person you want to notice you on the paper. Fold the paper and place inside the apple then add five apple seeds and all the honey and violet oil.

2. Place the top back on the apple and bind with the ribbon as you say:

   Goddess, heed my desire.
   Make the one I love feel my ardour.
   For the good of all, with harm to none,
   With free will, let there be love.

3. Place the apple somewhere dark (like in a cupboard) from the waxing to the full moon. On the full moon, take it out and bury it in the garden (or in a planter box if you have a balcony). Your love should notice you.

SPELL TO CROSS PATHS AGAIN WITH SOMEONE YOU CAN'T STOP THINKING ABOUT

Write their name on a bay leaf and add 1 drop of your blood. Burn the bay leaf in a candle flame, holding it by the stem as you chant:

Come to me, come to me, come to me.

You should see them again within three days.

FOR SOMEONE WHO IS SINGLE, LONELY AND READY FOR SOME LOVE ACTION!

Do this spell during the full moon, especially on a Friday night, which is ruled by Venus, the goddess of love.

You will need

- Piece of parchment or paper
- Feather quill
- Magickal ink (red Indian ink to which you have added 3 drops of your blood)
- Green cloth bag
- Vervain (for love and fidelity)
- Dried pink rose petals, which you've plucked yourself or have been given to you by a friend (for unconditional love)

1. On the parchment, use the quill and ink to inscribe the planetary symbol for Venus (♀), your initials and the infinity symbol (∞). Put the parchment in the bag with the vervain and rose petals.

2. Standing under the full moon, hold the charm bag in both hands close to your heart as you gaze at the moon and say:

Love be mine,
Love be mine,
Love be mine,
For all time.

3. Project all your desire for love into the bag. By the next full moon, things should be getting exciting!

DESIRE ME SPELL

This simple candle spell is not karma-free. I always say don't interfere with another's free will or your love spell will backfire. But if you don't care about this, then in the interests of 'freedom of information' here is a karma-loaded spell to make a certain person fall in love with you. Be careful what you wish for.

YOU WILL NEED

- Knife, for carving
- Red candle
- Patchouli essential oil
- Soil from the footprint of your desired one

1. Using the knife, carve the red candle with the initials of your desired one. Lick your thumb and anoint the carving with some of your saliva and a few drops patchouli oil. Around the base of the candle, sprinkle some of the soil you've collected.

2. Light the candle and focus on your desired one being with you. See yourselves together in each other's arms and beds. When the vision is strong, intone as many times as you like:

   Come to me, my will is great.
   Your fate with me you can't escape.

3. Repeat this ritual every night until the next full moon. They should be yours ... but it probably won't be what you expect!

Enchanted love that breaks the law of interfering with another's free will can have disappointing results. You may get the person only to find out they're not the charmed, ideal dream-lover you thought they were.

THE MAGICK OF ARABIC POETRY

Poetry held a special and revered place in medieval Arabian society; people often considered it to possess mystical, even magical, qualities. This belief stemmed from their deep appreciation for and understanding of the power of language, and the artistry of expression within Arab culture.

Here are some key aspects that contributed to poetry being perceived as magical.

Oral tradition

Poetry in medieval Arabia was primarily spoken out loud. Poets recited their verses in public gatherings, markets and courts, captivating audiences with their words. The rhythmic patterns and melodic cadences of poetry were mesmerising, creating an immersive experience for listeners.

Rhetorical skill

Poets were highly respected for their mastery of language and rhetoric. They could evoke emotions, convey complex ideas and capture the essence of human experiences through their verses. Their poetry's eloquence and craftsmanship was often viewed as evidence of divine inspiration or supernatural talent.

Healing and protection

People believed that poetry had healing properties and could be used to ward off evil spirits or bring blessings. Certain poetic verses, known as *ruqyah*, were recited for protection against harm or illness. People thought these verses possessed inherent power; they were often inscribed on amulets or written in calligraphy as protective talismans.

Love and romance

Love poetry held a special significance in Arabian culture. Through their verses, poets celebrated the beauty of their beloved, expressed their longing and desire, and immortalised the intensity of love. They believed the romantic imagery and emotive language of love poetry could enchant and captivate hearts.

Social influence

Poets wielded significant influence in medieval Arabian society. They were advisors to rulers, chroniclers of historical events and moral guides for the community. The words of a respected poet could sway public opinion, inspire loyalty or incite rebellion.

Connection to the divine

Poetry was often associated with spiritual enlightenment and divine inspiration. Poets were seen as conduits for transcendent truths, channelling insights from the unseen realm into the tangible realm of human experience. The act of composing or reciting poetry was considered to be a form of worship and way of communing with the divine.

People's belief in the magical power of poetry was rooted in their profound reverence for language, the expressive potential of art, and the cultural significance of storytelling and oral tradition. Through poetry, medieval Arabs sought to explore the mysteries of existence, celebrate the beauty of creation and connect with the ineffable aspects of the human spirit.

CAST AN ARABIC LOVE SPELL

Do this spell during the crescent moon. Familiarise yourself with the poem then perform the spell according to the instructions contained within it.

You will need

- Sand
- Damask roses (symbolising love and beauty)
- Oud (agarwood) incense (renowned for its rich and mystical aroma)
- Saffron threads (representing passion and vitality)
- Amethyst and moonstone crystals (for channelling the divine and enhancing poetic inspiration)
- Calligraphy quill and parchment (for inscribing verses with grace and precision)
- Lanterns adorned with intricate arabesque patterns (for illuminating the enchantment of the words)

1. Dress in white. Sprinkle a circle of sand then a circle of rose petals within it. State this spell aloud and perform:

> *Beneath the crescent moon's gentle glow,*
> *Desert sands whisper tales untold,*
> *Scatter blooms of damask rose,*
> *Its fragrance sweet, this love composed*
> *In the mist of oud's sacred smoke,*
> *It is love eternal I invoke.*
> *Before saffron's hue, like dawn's first light,*
> *This spell is woven in the still of night*

Let amethyst and moonstone's gleam,
Illuminate this poet's dream.
With every stroke of quill and ink,
Let magick flow, let our hearts sync. [Write your and/or your beloved's
name.]
With ardour this arabesque lantern shines
As words entwine, this love is mine.
With every line, passions rise
For in a poet's embrace, love does lie.
Like stars above in the heavens gleam,
Lovers live their eternal dreams.
So mote it be, this spell I cast,
In love's embrace, hearts hold fast.

By reciting a poem of love and intention - especially combining it with actions, crystals, scents and flowers - a true enchantment is manifested in the physical realm.

ARABIC LOVE CHARM

For centuries in Arabic culture, love charms have been used to attract love and affection. This charm is inspired by common cooking ingredients that are considered to have great power. You'll also want to write a rhyming Arabic love charm, because poetry is considered to have great magical power in Arabian culture.

YOU WILL NEED

- Frankincense resin (for its purifying properties and connection to spirituality)
- Cinnamon sticks (representing warmth, passion and love)
- Cardamom pods (desire and sensuality)
- Rose petals (symbolising love and passion)
- Cloves (attracting pure love and sincere friendship)
- Small red or pink velvet or tapestry pouch (for holding and carrying the charm)

1. Set a clear and positive intention. Focus on the type of love you desire whether it's self-love, romantic love or friendship.

2. Grind the frankincense resin into a fine powder. (Put it in the fridge for half an hour before you do this, which helps it grind evenly.) Crush the cinnamon sticks and cardamom pods. Keep the rose petals and cloves whole.

3. In a small bowl, mix the ground frankincense, cinnamon and cardamom with the rose petals and cloves. As you combine the elements, visualise your intention for love and positivity.

4. Hold the mixture in your hands and envision the charm being filled with the energy of love. Now it's time to chant your poetry (see 'Writing the charm', page 112) and charge the mixture.

5. Carefully place the charged mixture into the pouch. Tie three knots to secure the contents.

Notes

You can add a small personal item - such as a lock of hair, photograph or written affirmation - to further empower the charm.

Keep the charm close. Carry the sachet with you, place it in your bedroom or keep it somewhere you spend a significant amount of time. The charm symbolises your intention for love and positive energy, and draws that which you desire to you like a magnet.

Remember, the power of a love charm lies in the intention and belief behind it. Using this recipe as a starting point, feel free to adapt it based on your personal preferences and cultural context.

WRITING THE CHARM

This advice comes from an Arabian love poem composer I met in the desert, who spoke just enough English for me to piece this together:

When writing the charm, be sure to choose the right words. You want your charm to be sweet, romantic and heartfelt. Use phrases such as 'my love', 'my heart' and 'my soulmate' to convey your affection.

Consider the symbolism of certain objects and colours. Red is often associated with love and passion, while roses symbolise beauty and desire. Including these elements in your charm can add depth and meaning.

Personalise your charm. Use the name of the person you are trying to attract and include specific details about your feelings and desires.

Here is an example of an Arabic love charm:

Ya habibi, ya qalbi, ya roohi. Ana ahibbuki bshidda. Ana arju an takooni zawjati al-muqaddasah. Ahbabtuk min qalbi wa min jasad. Ya rabi al-'alamin, khalik lana hubban da'im wa mawaddah baina al-ashiqayn.

My love, my heart, my soul. I love you intensely. I hope you will be my holy spouse. I love you from my heart and my body. Oh Lord of the worlds, create for us eternal love and affection.

Use this poem for inspiration as you create your poetic charm. It doesn't have to be the best poem in the world, just the best you can do to sincerely project your love, and wishes for it to be returned, into the world.

DEEP LOVE SPELL TO ADD SPICE TO YOUR RELATIONSHIP

You will need

- Red pen
- 7 pieces parchment paper
- 7 pink candles

Fire of love oil

- 3 drops jasmine essential oil
- 2 drops rose geranium essential oil
- 1 drop orange essential oil
- 3 pinches cayenne pepper
- 1 pinch black pepper

Attraction powder

- 1 teaspoon dragon's blood powder
- 1 teaspoon allspice
- 1 teaspoon almond meal

1. On Friday night (the night of Venus), prepare the fire of love oil and attraction powder. Then write a letter of passion in red pen on the parchment. Include all the things you would like to do with your lover in a spicier relationship!

2. Anoint the candle with some of the oil and light it, standing it on the letter. Sprinkle the powder around the base of the candle in a sunwise direction (clockwise in the northern hemisphere, anticlockwise in the southern hemisphere) as you call your lover's name seven times.

3. Blow seven kisses to the candle and say:

   Mystic be the number seven
   With the touch that feels like heaven.
   This letter of my lust and love

I send to the ethers high above.
Bind to me spice and fun
So is my desire, so it must be done.

4. Leave the candle burning in a fire-safe holder throughout the night. In the morning, fold the letter around the powder and candle stub and keep in a box.

5. Repeat each night with a new candle and letter. By the following Friday - woo hoo! Watch out! Your sex life will be charmed!

CONJURING THE SENSUAL SELF WITH YLANG-YLANG

The rich, floral scent of ylang-ylang is associated with romance and sensuality. Ylang-ylang (*Cananga odorata*) is an essential oil derived from the flowers of the ylang-ylang tree, which is native to the rainforests of Southeast Asia, particularly in Indonesia, the Philippines and Malaysia.

Massaging with ylang-ylang can contribute to a heightened sensory experience, its alluring and exotic aroma making the massage more pleasurable and enjoyable. When incorporating ylang-ylang essential oil into a sensual massage, make sure you dilute it properly with a carrier oil to avoid skin irritation.

Here are some reasons why you should try ylang-ylang in a sensual massage.

Aphrodisiac properties

Ylang-ylang has aphrodisiac effects, meaning it can enhance romantic and sensual experiences. The heady scent has a positive influence on emotions and helps an individual open up to intimacy.

Calming and relaxing

The fragrance of ylang-ylang has calming and relaxing properties. When used in massage, it can help to reduce stress, anxiety and tension, creating a soothing environment that promotes a deeper connection between partners.

Balancing hormones

Aromatherapy practitioners say that ylang-ylang has a positive impact on hormonal balance. This can contribute to an increased sense of well-being and sensual mood during intimacy.

Skin benefits

Ylang-ylang essential oil should be diluted with a carrier oil such as sweet almond or jojoba oil before you apply it to the skin. This not only makes it safe for massage but also moisturises and nourishes the skin.

CONDOM SPELL

This spell was featured in my book: *Magickal Sex: Beds, Knobs and Broomsticks*. At the time (in 2006) it created quite an uproar. Most importantly, it confirms that safe sex is the most magickal sex!

1. To guarantee a successful night on the prowl, pick a condom (or two or three!) in your power colour. Maybe red for passion, black for mystery, blue for happiness or pink for love. Light a purple candle for success and burn musk incense for lust.

2. Hold the condoms in your hands and focus on your goal. In your mind's eye, see yourself meeting interesting, sexy people and

having your pick of the bunch! When the vision is clear, open your eyes, gaze at the candle flame and say:

> *Power of fire, heed my desire.*
> *My vision is clear – fuelled by desire.*
> *On this night, without delay,*
> *Passionate sex will come my way.*

3. Snuff the candle flame and say: 'So mote it be.' Pocket your condoms, head out and make sure you use them!

SEX SPELL

Before you perform this spell, decide with your lover what your goal is, such as money, success, career ... whatever. And remember as you do this ritual that all acts of love and pleasure are sacred to the goddess. This is a holy celebration of the sacred life force.

You will need

- 2 purple candles
- Goblet or chalice of champagne or sparkling mineral water
- Musk incense
- Flowers of passion (orange, red and tropical if possible)
- Galangal root powder, for sprinkling
- Sea salt, for sprinkling
- Cushions and rugs

1. Set up an altar with the candles, goblet of champagne (sacred to Erzulie, voodoo goddess of passion and love) or sparkling mineral water if you don't drink alcohol, musk incense, and your flowers of passion.

2. Sprinkle galangal and sea salt in a big circle. In the middle, place cushions and rugs for comfort!

3. The man stands in the north, the woman in the south. Both take a sip of champagne and stamp their feet and clap their hands as the woman says:

> *Man! Thou are potent and lusty.*
> *Come join with me my loins are afire!*

Then the man says:
> *Woman, thou art lovely and fertile.*
> *Come join with me so I may temper my sword in thy furnace.*

4. Stand looking at each other and let the erotic tension build ... then leap upon each other! Call out your goal when you are climaxing, for example: 'Money, money, money!' or 'Love, love, love!' Fuelled by your passion, it should manifest in the cosmos.

ORGASM MAGICK

Orgasm is a sacred and powerful gift of creation, not just a physical act. You can channel the intense energy and pleasure experienced during orgasm for positive intentions and connections.

Dedicate each beautiful experience to someone or something in your life or the universe you wish to honour and love. It's like taking all the joyful and passionate energy created during that intimate moment and directing it towards a specific purpose. It's a way of infusing the act with intention and significance beyond the immediate physical pleasure. By dedicating your orgasm to someone or something you love or wish to honour, this focused energy can have positive effects, whether it's strengthening relationships, promoting self-love, or sending positive energies into the universe.

Orgasm magick intertwines the physical and metaphysical, viewing the act of pleasure as a sacred opportunity to connect with the people and things that hold importance in your life. This personal and spiritual practice involves recognising the profound energy within the intimate, making it a meaningful and intentional experience beyond the physical sensations. In this age of Tinder and hook-ups, the act of sex and orgasm has lost much of its sacredness, so it's empowering and beautiful to reinvest in that.

To dedicate an orgasm, all you need to do as you feel the peak of climax approaching is to say a single word inside your head that describes where you want to send that healing ecstatic energy.

SMART SEX RITUAL TO HONOUR THE GOD AND GODDESS

You will need
- Red and pink candles (for love and passion)
- Musk and patchouli incense (for lust)
- Pink tiger-lily flowers or other opulent, pink, sweetly scented blooms
- Soft white feathers
- Vanilla bean ice cream (for happiness)
- Massage oil with ylang-ylang and rose geranium essential oils (pure aphrodisiacs)
- Pink, strawberry-flavoured condoms (for love and fun)

1. Set up your space by lighting candles and incense. Place the flowers in vases and scatter the feathers around so the area is opulent and inviting.

2. Honour the god/goddess within your lover by indulging them in sensual pleasures (all acts of love and pleasure are sacred to the goddess). Tickle them with feathers, eat ice cream off them, massage warm oil into their skin, maybe even drip some of the candle wax on them for extra excitement, and have fun using the condoms! The whole time be aware you are worshipping them, celebrating everything pure and holy about humanity - our divine sexuality!

TO SEE YOUR FUTURE HUSBAND

This spell is folklore from medieval times. Place a sprig of thyme in your left shoe and a sprig of rosemary in your right shoe on the Eve of St Agnes (20 January). You will have a vision of your future husband.

GYPSY GOOD-LUCK MARRIAGE SALTS

You will need

- ½ cup rock salt
- ½ cup finely ground white rice
- ½ cup coconut oil
- 2 handfuls gardenia petals (or similar white flower)
- 5 drops ylang-ylang essential oil

Mix all the ingredients together during a new moon and store in a cool, dark place until your wedding night. On this night, bathe with your partner in a tub into which the salts have been dispersed. This will ensure good luck and a happy start to your marriage.

HAPPINESS IN MARRIAGE

To herald a happy marriage, don't just exchange rings on the day, but exchange lockets with a photo and lock of each other's hair enclosed. You both snip your hair with scissors as you think about your love and desire for a happy marriage. The hair will hold your intent and work as a charm for your marriage.

TO TEST A LOVER'S FIDELITY

This is a medieval divination. To test the strength of your lover's feelings, tickle the inside of your nose with a yarrow leaf as you say:

Yarroway, yarroway, bear a white blow.
If my love loves me, my nose will bleed now.

TO STOP A PARTNER FROM BEING UNFAITHFUL

You will need

- White cloth
- Cotton, for stuffing
- Scissors
- Your partner's hair and nail clippings
- Red cord

1. Make a poppet. Cut a hole over the heart with scissors and place some of the unfaithful one's hair and nail clippings in there. Sew it up. Holding the doll in both hands, say: 'I name thee [name of person].'

2. Take the red cord and wrap it firmly around the doll, binding the legs, arms, mouth and groin as you say:

   I bind thee true, no lies to be,
   I break the chain of deceit.
   No love in vain, my will is spun,
   A binding charm, the pledge is done.
   Betrayal's grip, I firmly thwart,
   With loyalty you shall now walk.
   I bind thee now, in sacred verse.
   No unfaithful step, no love adverse,
   May this enchantment tightly cling,
   Of fidelity your heart shall sing.

3. When you have finished, hold the doll in both hands and say: 'This I declare for the good of all. So mote it be.' If you can, put the doll under your partner's bed.

Note: another way to do a binding spell is to repeat a simple mantra as you bind the doll. For example, it would be appropriate to repeat the following as you wrap the poppet:

I bind thee now, in sacred verse,
No unfaithful step, no love adverse.

FOR BREAKING UP A LOVE AFFAIR SO YOU CAN GET BACK WITH YOUR PARTNER

Take a picture of your lover, cross it with garlic and a drop of honey (to lessen the pain), and bury it under a tree. It will then be easy to end the affair.

Remember, in all matters of the heart, you should act practically as well as magickally. Approach matters of the heart with a balanced perspective. Burying a crossed picture with garlic and honey under a tree serves as a cathartic ritual, but it's equally crucial to address the root causes of the affair. Why did you have the affair?

Take time to reflect on the reasons behind your actions. Was it a lack of emotional fulfilment, communication issues or external pressures? Understanding your underlying motivations can provide valuable insights for personal growth and relationship development.

Consider having open and honest communication with your partner. If the relationship is causing distress, discuss your feelings, concerns and desires. Seek the assistance of a relationship counsellor or therapist to navigate the complexities.

Magick is a tool that complements practical efforts. While rituals can aid in emotional release and magickal actions can align energies between the worlds for action in the physical plane, they shouldn't replace genuine communication and self-reflection. Use both practical and magickal means to heal, grow and make informed decisions about your relationships.

Ultimately, fostering a healthy and respectful approach to relationships involves addressing issues with practical actions and thoughtful introspection ... and a generous sprinkle of magick!

TO GET SEX HAPPENING AGAIN

You will need

- Lush tropical flowers
- Patchouli and cinnamon essential oils (male aphrodisiacs) or ylang-ylang essential oil (female aphrodisiac)
- Salt
- Rugs and cushions
- Almond oil

1. Create a sexy environment. Decorate the room with the tropical flowers and burn patchouli and cinnamon or ylang-ylang oils. Sprinkle a large circle of salt and place rugs and cushions within.

2. In a bowl, blend some almond oil with a few drops of patchouli oil. Invite your partner into the sacred circle and stand facing each other. Slowly each of you removes your clothing - do this sensually and confidently - connecting with a sincere desire to improve your relationship. Dip your fingers into the oil and stroke each other lightly.

3. The following is based on a medieval charm - but feel free to create other charms that reflect your taste and pleasures. The words must be sincere. Fun and laughter are great ways to connect and also release tension and fear. The man says this charm:

Woman, thou art fertile and lush.
Come join with me, my loins are afire!

Then the woman says:

Man, thou art strong and potent.
Impale me upon thy lusty sword!

4. Leap on each other! All acts of love and pleasure are sacred to the goddess, so after you've made love, stay in the sacred circle and allow the energies to continue circulating. Offer these energies for the bettering of positive intimacy for all humans.

SPELL FOR NO LIBIDO

YOU WILL NEED

- 1 red candle
- Knife, for carving
- Lavender essential oil
- Warm honey

1. Before bed, take the red candle and warm the wax by dipping it in boiling water. Carve five notches down one side, each about half a centimetre apart. Massage lavender oil into the candle and light it. Gazing into the flame, place a drop of honey on your tongue as you say:

   Honey sweet, light within me.
   Passion for life, sweet and sexy.

2. Do this five times then gaze into the flame, feeling the warm rush of passion move through you until the candle has burned down to the first notch. Snuff the flame. Repeat the ritual for four more nights. By then you will have no problem being in touch with your sensuous self.

   Note: it's a good idea to start this spell on a Monday, which is ruled by the moon and aligned with your cycles of femininity.

By Friday, which is ruled by Venus the planet of sensuous love, you will be ripe for some sensual weekend expression and adventure!

> ### MORE TIPS
>
> - For women: regular bathing in a warm bath with 11 drops lemon balm essential oil will ignite sensual passion and the ability to receive love.
> - For men: regular bathing in a warm bath with 4 drops cypress, 4 drops patchouli and 3 drops cinnamon essential oils will enhance virility.

MEDIEVAL SPELL TO HEAL A BROKEN HEART

In the medieval era, the landscape of magic was expansive, with various practitioners engaging in different forms of mystical arts. Individuals from diverse backgrounds such as monks, priests, physicians, surgeons, midwives, folk healers and diviners all participated in what was considered magick. A pivotal yet often overlooked aspect of this rampant magickal expression of the time was the contribution of the women who, in their magickal practices, unknowingly sowed the seeds for the emergence of the witch. Yet for this, they would ultimately be persecuted by the very priests who they practised their healing arts alongside.

The magical practices of this era often involved using medicinal herbs for healing purposes, blurring the lines between classical medicine and mystical elements. The practitioners - whether monks, physicians or folk healers - incorporated charms and potions into their methods, hoping to dispel sickness and restore health. In this intricate web of magical beliefs and practices, opinions on what constituted magic varied greatly. Little did many know, especially the women involved, that their magical pursuits (for which they would suffer so greatly) would play a noble role in laying the foundation for the empowering spiritual movement of witchcraft that emerged in later centuries.

Despite how complex and far-reaching the burgeoning magical practices were, people's needs of the medieval world were often simple ... and the same as they are today. Love always needed a cure or was a sickness to be healed. This simple, powerful spell would have worked to heal a broken heart.

You will need

- 1 white candle
- Rose petals
- Piece of parchment (or paper)
- Quill with ink pot (or a pen)
- Lavender essential oil

1. Light the candle and place it in front of you. Sprinkle rose petals around the candle.

2. On the parchment, write the name of the person whose heart needs healing. Sprinkle a few drops of lavender oil on the paper.

3. Holding the paper with both hands, close your eyes. Visualise the person standing in front of you, smiling and happy. Chant the following spell three times:

   By the power of the moon and stars above,
   I call upon the goddess of love.
   Heal this heart, mend it well,
   Blessed by this enchanting spell.

4. Burn the paper in the candle flame. Let the candle burn out on its own.

Remember, this spell is only meant to heal a broken heart. It cannot force someone to love you or another person to change their feelings. Use it or offer it with pure intentions and an open heart.

GETTING RID OF ITEMS AFTER A RELATIONSHIP ENDS

When the remnants of a relationship linger like ominous shadows, you can face the dilemma of what to do with the tangible memories that remain. Whether you're burdened by guilt, seeking closure or striving to reclaim the positive essence of cherished items, a cleansing ritual can be a powerful way to release the past and pave the way for new beginnings.

This ritual offers a sacred space to untangle emotional threads, whether you're grappling with guilt, navigating a one-sided break-up, or seeking to make cherished items feel like just yours again.

You WILL NEED
- Items bearing the weight of memories
- Firepit or space for a bonfire
- White ribbon
- Sprigs of fresh basil
- Eucalyptus or sage leaves
- Shovel or spade

1. Gather the items you wish to cleanse or remove from your life. Build a substantial fire in a fireplace, firepit or outside in a clear and open space.

2. As you stand before the cleansing fire, acknowledge your emotions. Observe where you feel blocked in your body. Breathe deeply, allowing each breath to release tension, pain or regrets.

3. Wrap each item in some white ribbon, a symbol of purity and the potential for a clean slate. Bind a sprig of basil with the

bundle, invoking its cleansing properties and ability to foster new perspectives.

4. Sprinkle with eucalyptus or sage leaves to release a cleansing fountain of smoke. Gaze upon the flames, listening to the crackling of the leaves and feeling the energy of transformation ripe in the air.

5. Hold each wrapped item over the fire, allowing the cleansing smoke to envelop it. With each pass, speak the words:

    I release you without malice or guilt.
    The past is gone, tears no longer spilled.

6. Feel the weight of the past lifting and ties loosening as the smoke purifies the items from the energies of the past.

7. Gently drop each bundle you don't wish to keep into the fire, watching as the flames consume the physical representations of your memories. Witness the alchemy of transformation in your life.

8. Once reduced to ashes, collect any non-biodegradable elements then turn the ashes into the earth with the shovel or spade. Feel the connection to our cycles of nature, letting things die to nurture new growth.

In this ritual of cleansing and release, experience solace in the knowledge that you've honoured the past, yet opened the door to the possibilities lying ahead.

TO GET RID OF AN EX-PARTNER BOTHERING YOUR NEW LOVER

Write their name on a piece of paper and place in an ice-cube tray with 1 rusty nail and 3 peppercorns. Cover with water and put it in the freezer as you say: 'Be gone from our life, so there is no strife.' They will stay away.

If you really need to boost this spell, carve their initials into 9 garlic cloves with a sharp knife. Plant the cloves across your front driveway or the entrance to your home. Like a vampire, they won't be able to step over the line of garlic.

TO GET RID OF BAD FEELINGS TOWARDS A PARTNER'S EX

Recognise that your partner is who they are because of their previous life before you. Honour and respect their previous experiences as being an integral part of them. Rather than focusing on the ex and feeling insecure, do this ritual.

YOU WILL NEED

- 1 white candle
- White flowers (like roses or lilies for example)
- Mandarin essential oil

1. Light a white candle and surround it with white flowers, perhaps roses or lilies.
2. Diffuse some mandarin oil for happiness and clarity and say this love charm poem. Remember, poetry is powerful love magick - feel free to write your own inspired by the following words:

   In liberty's embrace, my thoughts unwind
   From envy's chains, my heart inclines.

Love, a radiant guide, casts all jealous storms aside.
In the clarity of my unshackled mind,
Dreams blossom free, no shadows bind.
Passion, a distracting flame untold,
Serene is my life – in love's stronghold.

Repeat this charm as often as you need to.

TO CHANGE YOUR LUCK IN FINDING SOMEONE TO LOVE

Carry a sprig of yarrow close to your heart. The herb yarrow is traditionally used in love spells; in the 19th century, it was considered to be the first herb the baby Jesus picked, so it's good for luck.

A LOVE SPELL TO ENCOURAGE PERFECT LOVE

If you keep dating the wrong people, this spell will help to make sure your new love affair will be a perfect love for you. It will grow all that is best and positive about this new union. Scoop some soil from the left footprint of your new lover. (Don't let them see you doing this or you may scare them off!) Sprinkle this on top of some dark soil in a little flowerpot and plant some marigolds or whatever your favourite flower is (roses are a good choice too). As you water the growing plant say:

My heart is ready for true company.
May this love be perfect for me.

Stay attentive to your plant and your new partner - relax and trust that this relationship can grow like your plant.

YOU WANT YOUR BOSS TO FALL IN LOVE WITH YOU

Now, you can't make a specific person fall in love with you - it will always backfire. It breaks a basic witch's law: 'Do what you want but don't interfere with another's free will.'

YOU WILL NEED

- Piece of paper
- Knife, for carving
- 1 pink candle

1. Write a detailed letter about what qualities of your boss turn you on. Don't think of your boss's face, just picture a stranger with those qualities.

2. Carve your name into one side of the pink candle and the word 'Love' on the other side. Lick your thumb and trace over your name with your saliva to make it your own.

3. Read your letter aloud by the light of the candle every night for seven nights leading up to the full moon. By the full moon, a new man with those qualities should have entered your life.

WARNING: WHAT IF YOUR BOSS LIKES YOU TOO?

Here is some practical advice about why you may not want to magickally (or practically) encourage this love match.

Dating in the workplace can introduce complexities that impact both the personal and professional spheres. While workplace relationships aren't inherently wrong, they often come with challenges. Navigating the thin line between personal and professional boundaries can potentially lead to conflicts of interest or favouritism. Moreover, if the relationship takes a turn for the worse, you may find yourself in an uncomfortable or hostile work environment. Maintaining professionalism is crucial, and the risk of gossip or rumours can undermine your reputation. By avoiding workplace romance, you can foster a more focused and harmonious professional atmosphere, preserving your personal relationships and career trajectory.

It can be really hard to not fall for someone you work with, especially when you see them every day and you're looking for a way to find a slightly boring job more interesting. Alternatively, your job might be amazing and the person you're working with is also amazing so you feel like you have this connection! But in more than 30 years of reading tarot and offering divination services for people, one of the biggest areas where people ask for help is in work relationships, where they've crossed the line and are in an intimate relationship with someone they work with. It's often so very difficult.

Considering all this, it's definitely better to do a love spell where you don't specify a person, especially a boss or coworker, and let the universe grow your life expansively and open up your circle of human connections. That way, you're more likely to experience an evolved and uplifting relationship, one that elevates your experience on this planet.

LGBTQIA+ MAGICK

Gays and lesbians have special magickal totems:

Hyacinth

The sacred flower for homosexual men is the hyacinth. The ancient Greek god Apollo, also sacred for gay men, loved young boys and fell in love with a young Spartan prince named Hyacinthus. One day, they were both throwing discus in the gymnasium when the discus hit a stone. It rebounded and hit Hyacinthus in the head, killing him. Apollo was distraught; he turned Hyacinthus's body into a flower to make him immortal.

Anointing the oil of the flower on the skin, or drying the petals and carrying them with you, will affirm the masculinity of gay men and give them Apollo's special protection.

Cypress

The cypress tree is also sacred to gay men. Another of Apollo's lovers, Cyparissus, was playing with his pet stag and accidently killed it with a spear. Broken-hearted, he asked Apollo to kill him so he could be with his stag. Apollo was touched but couldn't bear to lose him forever, so turned him into a cypress tree.

Cypress represents love transcending difficulty, torment and death. You can anoint yourself with the oil, burn it as incense or plant a cypress by the door of a home to bless its inhabitants.

Rose

The rose is the sacred flower for lesbians. It is sacred to Aphrodite, the ancient Greek goddess of love and beauty. Sappho, the legendary lesbian poet of ancient Greece, called the rose the 'queen of the flowers'. Roses of all colours are sacred to lesbians: red for lust, pink for love, white for fidelity and health, and yellow for wisdom.

Lesbians making a commitment to their partnership can exchange emerald rings anointed with rose oil to bless their union with love and beauty. You can also prick each other's thumb with a rose thorn and mix a drop of each other's blood in wine, drinking to declare your love for each other in the eyes of the goddess.

RAINBOW SPELL FOR STRONG PERSONAL IDENTITY AND CONFIDENCE

Here's a positive and empowering spell to help an LGBTQI person strengthen their personal identity and boost their confidence. This spell emphasises self-love, acceptance and celebrating your unique identity.

You will need

- 1 rainbow-coloured candle or several candles in rainbow colours
- Small mirror
- Piece of paper
- Bowl of salt water
- Small crystal or gemstone representing confidence (citrine or tiger's eye)
- Empowering essential oil or fragrance (could be a blend or your favourite perfume or cologne)

1. Create a quiet, comfortable space where you won't be disturbed. Make it attractive with cushions and throws.

2. Arrange the candle(s) in front of you, along with the spell items you are using. If using essential oil, anoint the candle(s) with a drop, or you can kiss the candle(s) before you light them.

3. Light the rainbow candle(s) as you say:

    I honour the vibrant expression of my identity.

4. Take some deep breaths and close your eyes. Visualise a warm, radiant sphere of light surrounding you, covering you with love and acceptance. Open your eyes and look into the mirror. Smile at your reflection and say:

    I am proud of who I am. I embrace my true self with love and confidence.

5. On the paper, write down positive affirmations about your identity and confidence. Things like:

    I am worthy of love and respect.
    I embrace my uniqueness and celebrate my identity.
    I am confident in my true self.

6. Hold the paper with the affirmations in your hand, letting the candlelight shine upon it. Recite each affirmation aloud, slowly and clearly. Visualise the words glowing with light and energy, enveloping you and becoming part of you.

7. Dip the crystal into the bowl of salt water to cleanse it of any negativity. Then hold it in both hands to your heart. Imagine it absorbing positive energy and the affirmations. Say:

    May this crystal be a beacon of my confidence and a reminder of my strength.

8. Hold it above the candle flame to charge it with the light and energy of the candle(s). Say:

    With the power of light and love, I seal this spell.
    I am confident, I am strong, I am beautifully me.

9. Spend a few moments holding the crystal and gazing into the flames, seeing your path forward bathed with positivity and good fortune.

10. When you are ready, blow out the candle(s) to blow away any obstacles of self-doubt from your path. Keep the crystal with you as a talisman of confidence and personal strength.

POSITIVE LOVE SPELL USING MOON WATER ENERGIES

Harnessing the energy of moon water has been a valued practice in many cultures since the Middle Ages, especially in Eastern Europe. Working with moon water is potent and can help you attract love in a positive way.

The best time to do this spell is during a new or full moon, ensuring the moonlight can shine into your water. The new moon phase is ideal for new beginnings and attracting love, while the full moon gives an even more powerful boost.

You will need
- Clear container filled with spring water
- Dark-coloured cloth

1. Take the container outside under the moonlight. Hold the container over your head and try to see the moonlight reflecting through the water. When you can see it, bow to the moon three times in respect and gratitude. Chant positive affirmations or a loving mantra that resonates with your intentions for attracting love.

2. Return inside with the container, keeping all the lights turned off to maintain the moon's energy. Wrap the container in the cloth and leave it to sit for one week to fully infuse with the moon's energy.

3. When it is ready, you can add moon water to your daily routine: use it in your bath, or sprinkle it around your living space to attract positive and loving energies into your life.

SPECIAL NOTE FOR THE LGBTQI COMMUNITY

This spell's positive energies are perfectly aligned for the LGBTQI community, who are often ostracised in our predominantly heteronormative world. The gentle, supportive and accepting love of lunar energies resonates deeply with those seeking affirmation and genuine connection. By embracing these energies, you can attract a fulfilling love that also respects and celebrates your true self.

Remember, when casting love spells:

POSITIVE INTENTIONS	Ensure your intentions are pure and focused on attracting love in a positive, consensual and respectful manner.
NO MANIPULATION	This spell should not be used to manipulate or control anyone.
RESPECT FREE WILL	Always respect the free will of others. True love comes from mutual respect and genuine connection.

By keeping these things in mind, you can cast a love spell that aligns with positive energies and fosters genuine, loving connections. The most powerful spells come from a place of love and respect for yourself and others.

HOW TO REVIVE A DYING LOVE USING LOVE SPELLS

Love spells can be a powerful way to revive a fading relationship, especially when it has been impacted by gender confusion or misunderstandings. This positive, gender-neutral love spell uses objects, oils and herbs aligned with love magic to rekindle the bond between you and your partner.

YOU WILL NEED

- Photograph of you and your partner together in happy times
- Rose quartz (symbolising love)
- Dried rose petals (for love and passion)
- 1 pink candle (representing love and affection)
- Lavender essential oil (for calm and healing)
- 2 pieces of paper
- Fireproof dish
- Small bowl of water
- Small pouch or envelope

1. Create an altar by arranging the photograph, rose quartz and dried rose petals in a circle. Anoint the candle with lavender oil, place in the centre of your altar and light it.

2. On the first piece of paper, write your past problems - let them pour out. Fold the paper as many times as possible until the problems are tightly contained.

3. Light the folded paper using the candle's flame, then place it in the fireproof dish to burn completely. As it burns, focus on releasing past confusions and misunderstandings, allowing space for renewed love and connection.

4. Pick up the rose quartz in both hands, hold it to your heart, and focus on the love and connection you wish to revive.

5. On the second piece of paper, describe the love you wish to rekindle and the qualities you cherish in your partner. Be specific and heartfelt. Place the paper under the bowl of water.

6. Hold the photograph and say the following affirmation:

   May the love between us be revived and strengthened, clear of confusion, and full of forgiveness and acceptance.

7. Visualise you and your partner being happy, understanding and loving each other even more deeply for the problems you've learned from.

8. Dip your fingers in the bowl, which is now infused with the words you've written, and sprinkle it around the photograph and rose petals.

9. Allow the candle to burn out on its own. Place the rose quartz and paper in a pouch or envelope and place under your pillow or on your altar to magnify the love potential between you.

Ways to add to the spell

- Each day, take a moment to hold the rose quartz and read the paper you wrote, focusing on positive and loving thoughts about your relationship.
- Show appreciation for your partner's efforts and uniqueness. Go on dates, share secrets, and ask for their opinions to rebuild trust and intimacy.
- Small gifts and thoughtful gestures can help to keep the love alive and show your partner how much you care.

RITUAL INSPIRED BY SIWA FOR BLESSING SAME-SEX RELATIONSHIPS

Located in Egypt's Western Desert, the Siwa Oasis is renowned not only for its stunning natural beauty and ancient ruins, but also for its unique cultural history. Before the Arab influence brought more conservative views on sexuality, Siwa was notable for its acceptance and normalisation of same-sex relationships among men. This cultural openness was reflected in social practices and rituals where these relationships were celebrated and even institutionalised through ceremonial marriages.

The following ritual to bless same-sex relationships is inspired by Siwa and is perfect to perform with your partner. It is best performed in a quiet outdoor space where you can connect with the natural elements.

You will need

- Small altar or sacred space
- Sticks of incense (such as frankincense and myrrh for grounding and protection)
- Small bowl
- Piece of white clay
- Salt rock crystals
- Small container of warm sand
- Dates
- Olives
- Piece of parchment paper

1. Set up your altar, arranging the ritual items on it. Sit opposite your partner and synchronise your breaths, slowly breathing in and out together. Both take a stick of incense and light it from the same flame.

2. Stand and together sprinkle some of the salt around the circle to purify and connect with the natural indigenous elements of Siwa as you say in unison:

   May this salt cleanse and renew our bond, bringing deeper clarity and peace.

3. Both hold a piece of white clay in your hands, feeling its cool, grounding energy. Say:

   We honour the earth energies of Siwa, grounding and strong, to bless and protect our love.

4. Pick up handfuls of the warm sand, taking a moment to feel the flowing texture and connect with its energy. Say:

   This warm sand represents the flowing love between us.

5. Entwining your arms, eat one date each and say:

   This sacred date blesses the sweetness of our love.

6. Now eat an olive each and say:

   This olive blesses the endurance of our love.

7. Finally say together:

   As dates and olives nourish the body, may our love nourish our souls.

8. On the parchment, both write down your intentions for your relationship. Be specific about your desires for love, harmony, protection and spiritual connection as well as any plans you may have together for the future.

9. Hold the paper together and read the contents twice. Then fold three times. Keep this paper in a safe and sacred place with some of the sand and salt.

10. To finish, thank the natural elements and any spiritual guides or ancestors that may have come through during the ritual. Say:

    With gratitude, we honour the earth, the elements and the spirit of Siwa. Our love is blessed and protected.

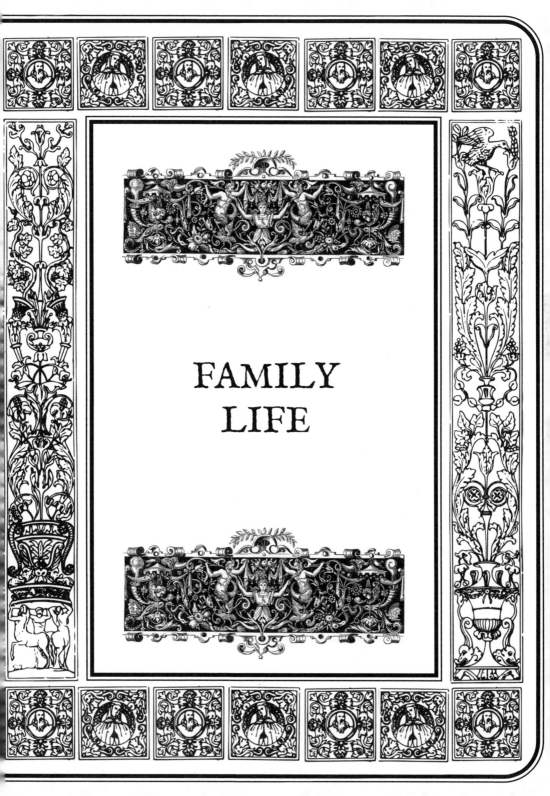

FAMILY
LIFE

ENCHANT YOUR FUTURE BLOODLINE

This is a generous and benevolent spell to enchant the lives of your descendants with good health, abundant fortune, great love and joy. It will help position them to make a positive difference on this planet and safeguard the future of humanity, physically and spiritually.

You will need

- 1 candle
- Incense of your choice
- Pen with permanent ink
- Recycled paper or parchment
- Special box or container

1. To weave this spell, first seek a tranquil sanctuary where you can meditate undisturbed. Light a candle and incense then settle into the sacred space, closing your eyes and breathing deeply. Visualise your future generations - they may appear as faces and bodies or as shadows of potential. See their lives filled with joy, love and fulfilment. See them spreading kindness and positivity, impacting the world in wondrous ways. Tap into your feelings as you consider this outcome of your existence while being in the physical plane now.

2. When you are resonating with a deep emotional connection, open your eyes and, using the pen, inscribe your wish on recycled paper or parchment. Describe what you saw in your mind's eye during your meditation of manifestation.

3. Fold the paper three times and hold it to your heart, stating this charm:

> *For the good of all with all the magic within me,*
> *I cast this spell for my future bloodline to be.*
> *May their health, fortune and love be blessed,*

Their lives filled with joy beyond measure, awake and at rest.
May they be the beacons of hope, the harbingers of change,
Guided by resilience, their progress shall evolve and prevail.
May their spirits be strong and their hearts be pure,
Led by light in their hearts that forever endures.
So mote it be.

4. Repeat the incantation three times with the paper held to your heart. It is now empowered with your life's pulse.

5. Place it with care and love in a sacred box to keep somewhere secret and safe, or place it on your altar.

Remember, the fusion of your intention, belief and sincerity is the fuel that infuses your spell. Trust in the universe's power to manifest your desires in divine timing and have faith that your future generations shall thrive with abundance and joy.

INVITE A NEW BABY INTO YOUR LIFE

Skyclad (naked) and under a full moon, rub 6 drops jasmine essential oil diluted into ¼ cup jojoba or olive oil onto your belly. With your hands still streaked with the sacred oil, run them over a silver candle. Light the candle, hold it up to the moon and say:

Mother goddess of the moon
Bless me with your fruitful glow.
As I stand in your ripe light
May a loving soul enter me tonight.

Carry the candle inside, being careful not to let the flame blow out, then make love with your partner in the candlelight. When you are finished, snuff the flame and start making plans for a baby!

TO HELP CONCEIVE A BABY

Try this old European trick: bind 11 or 13 coriander seeds to your left thigh before making love. Increase your husband's libido by adding crushed coriander seeds to his morning coffee.

SPELL TO HELP CONCEIVE A GIRL

No fertility or childbirth ritual is going to work if you doubt its ability. Simply 'following instructions' and wearing a piece of rose quartz in a bracelet on your wrist probably won't help you conceive unless you understand why it's powerful in this situation, why it's aligned to your goal. The key to unlocking magick in your life is to have a relationship with the magick, to 'co-create' with the universe.

The best time to do this spell is during the waxing moon when its gentle crescent appears low in the sunset sky.

You WILL NEED

- Pink paper
- 1 pink candle
- Dried chamomile flowers
- Fireproof dish
- Feather

1. Write a girl's name on the paper if you have a perfect one chosen; if not, write the word 'girl'. Light the candle as you say:
   Sacred flame, light the way for a little girl to come and stay.

2. As you repeat the charm, fold the paper into a little pouch and fill it with the chamomile.

3. Light the corner of the paper pouch with the candle flame, place on the fireproof dish and allow it to burn. Use the feather to make intuitive signals with the smoke - a message to the female spirit you wish to enter your life. Keep repeating the charm until you feel she has heard you.

4. When the pouch and flowers are ash, sprinkle them over a growing plant to add extra 'growth' energy to your spell.

Note: Be fire-safe when you do this spell.

SPELL TO CONCEIVE A BOY

To conceive a boy, use blue paper, blue candle and a flower bud (any flower) in place of the pink paper, candle and chamomile in the previous spell. Say this charm:

Sacred flame, light the way for a little boy to come and stay.

Write a boy's name or the word 'boy' on the paper. When you fan the feather, send the symbols to a male spirit.

FOR A CALM PREGNANCY

Diffuse aromatherapy oils in your home, such as a blend of lavender and sandalwood essential oils when you want to feel grounded, or rose geranium and bergamot oils when you need a pickup.

Never use clary sage essential oil when pregnant; it can cause uterine contractions so is contraindicated in pregnancy.

Burn a pale blue candle next to a single gardenia in a crystal vase and invoke the ancient Greek goddess Hestia, asking her to help you and your baby grow in peace together. You can invite Hestia close by keeping a candle burning safely in the kitchen. She is the goddess of hearth, home and family, and is drawn to where there is light in the heart of the home.

FOR A TROUBLE-FREE PREGNANCY

Wear a bracelet featuring bloodstone on your left arm as protection against miscarriage. Then when it's time for your baby to be born, switch it to your right to support an easy delivery.

Drink infusions of peppermint, ginger and lemon balm tea during your first trimester to ease queasiness.

When you are ready to give birth, drink raspberry leaf tea and diffuse clary sage essential oil in a burner.

Under each full moon of your pregnancy, massage a blend of neroli and almond essential oils into your stomach in a sunwise direction (clockwise in the northern hemisphere, anticlockwise in the southern hemisphere) as you say:

Bless me, mother moon,
Fill me with elation.
As I join with you
On this journey of creation.

RELAXATION RITUAL
BEFORE HAVING A BABY

Find a favourite spot in nature where you feel safe and can visit every day for 15 minutes. (If you only have a balcony, buy a beautiful, lush plant to sit next to.) When in your spot, place your hands gently over your stomach and breathe with your baby - soon they will be in your arms enjoying their first fresh breaths. Make sure you bring them to your special place in nature and breathe together. Their life will be charmed and blessed.

YOU WILL NEED

- Pale purple or blue silk
- Lavender and chamomile flowers
- Rosewood essential oil
- 1 moonstone crystal

1. Create a charm pillow by making a pouch with the silk. Stuff the pouch with the lavender and chamomile, 4 drops rosewood essential oil and the moonstone.

2. Carry the charm pillow with you when you sit in your special place. Press it to release the divine scent and qualities of the herbs and oils. As you breathe deeply, repeat this charm at least seven times:

> *Peaceful is my natural state.*
> *My baby grows inside me and I wait*
> *For our time to meet face to face,*
> *Trusting in our divine and blessed fate.*

SPELL FOR AN OVERDUE BABY

Note: don't cross your legs (an old witch's tale)!

You will need

- 1 orange candle
- Small bell or gong
- Raspberry leaf tea
- Clary sage essential oil
- Oil burner
- Jojoba oil

1. Facing east at sunrise, light an orange candle (for release and success), the colour of the womb chakra. Strike the bell three times and as you repeat:

   By the power of three
   Bring forth this life,
   Now ripe within me.

2. Strike the bell three times again and snuff the candle. Do this every morning until the baby comes (which won't be long!). Drink raspberry leaf tea throughout the day (check with your doctor first). As you drink the tea, visualise your womb as a vibrant orange colour.

3. Use clary sage oil in your oil burner. Dilute 3 drops clary sage in 1 teaspoon jojoba oil. Mix and massage in clockwise circles on your stomach.

   Note: please check with your doctor before using clary sage oil, which is contraindicated during pregnancy but can help ease labour pains and encourage uterine contractions.

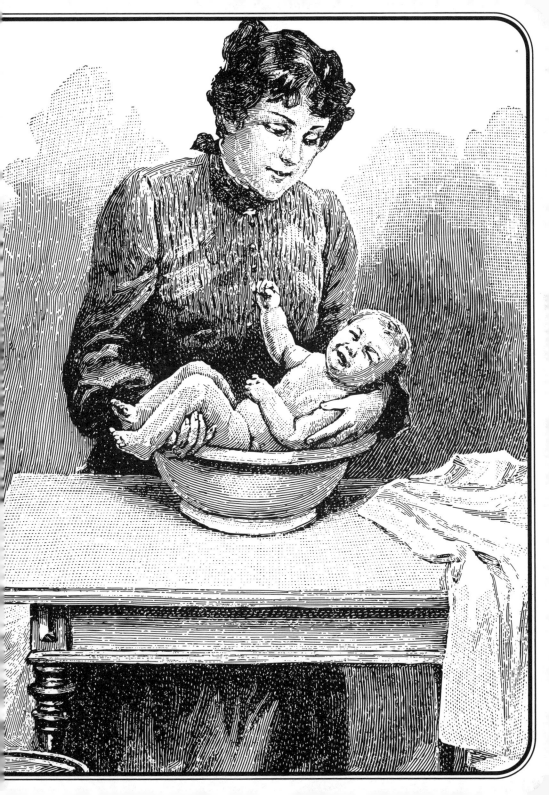

WITCH'S BLESSING FOR NEWBORNS AND YOUNG CHILDREN

You will need

- White daisies
- Flaxseeds (linseeds)
- Piece of elderwood or elderflowers
- Piece of cedarwood
- Lavender flowers
- Rosemary leaves
- Mortar and pestle
- Charcoal disc
- Crystal or glass bowl
- Spring water
- Rose quartz crystal
- Knife, for carving
- White candle
- Lavender essential oil

1. Decorate your baby's cot or bed with white daisies or a similar white-blossomed flower. The night before performing this ritual, sprinkle a circle of flaxseeds around their sleeping area to protect and begin the blessing.

2. Bathe your baby in a warm bath with a piece of elderwood in it. (Alternatively, place a handful of elderflower blossoms in a muslin bag and float it in the water.)

3. Burn incense made of 2 parts cedarwood, 2 parts lavender and 1 part rosemary. Grind these in a mortar and pestle and burn on a charcoal disc, or just throw handfuls of the mixture on an open fire.

4. Set up a small altar with a crystal bowl of spring water in which you have placed a piece of rose quartz. Carve your baby's name on the white candle and trace over it with some lavender oil.

5. Hold your baby in your arms as you say:

    [Name], you are held in the embrace of the Lady and Lord.
    May your life be charmed and free from harm,
    And all the blessings of the universe be bestowed upon you.

6. Sprinkle a little of the spring water on her head as you say:

    Blessed is [Name] by sacred water and earth.

7. Fan a little of the incense smoke over your baby as you say:

    Blessed is [Name] by sacred fire and air.

8. Seal your blessing with the witches' sacred words:

    So mote it be.

9. Have a celebratory party to honour your child's blessing. Plant a patch of iris on the day of your baby's blessing ceremony. You can do this as a part of the above rite. As the flowers grow, so will your child's well-being and happiness.

Note: feel free to elaborate on this rite and include words and actions that are meaningful to you. As a part of the ceremony, you might like to write a letter to your child expressing your love, hopes and dreams for them. Seal the letter with wax and place in a safe chamber until the child's 16th birthday. On this day, hold a 'rites of maturing' blessing ceremony when the child can break the seal, open the letter and read it.

TIPS FOR HAPPY BABIES

- Hang a mulberry leaf above your baby's cot for protection.
- Add ½ cup chamomile tea to the milk in your baby's bottle with a little honey for sweetness to soothe your baby.

- The juice of the milkweed herb (press the leaves and stem to release) can be anointed on your baby's third eye (between the eyebrows) upon waking to enhance their imagination and creativity.
- Add parsley to your baby's bathwater for protection.

A SLEEP SPELL SACHET

YOU WILL NEED
- Muslin
- Dried rose petals
- Dried mint
- Crushed cloves

In a muslin sachet combine the rose petals, mint and cloves, then hang the sachet over your child's bed. At bedtime, crush the sachet with your hand, agitating the contents as you say: 'I weave a charm of peace so you, my love, will sleep.'

TIPS TO HELP BABIES SLEEP AT NIGHT

Use pale blue sheets and sleeping wear.
Prepare a weak infusion of cool chamomile and mint herbal tea before sleep. (Check with the doctor first.)
Use lavender essential oil in an oil burner.

TODDLERS BEWARE!

If a toddler is the first person to touch a newly planted thyme plant, they will remain single for life! I'm not sure where this came from, or its validity, but don't risk it!

TO HELP A YOUNG CHILD WHO IS SCARED OF MONSTERS FALL ASLEEP

If you can't convince your child that the monsters they fear don't exist, make a circle of salt and crushed sage leaves around their bed. Salt is for protection and sage gets rid of evil spirits. When the child is in bed, sprinkle this mixture around them, reassuring them that nothing can get to them.

The following morning, vacuum or sweep up the mixture and place it in the garden far away from the child's bedroom. Sprinkle fresh mixture every night.

Make an altar with your child to watch over them while they sleep. Include a beautiful picture of a goddess, a vase of flowers and a rose quartz crystal. Add any favourite superhero dolls on the altar to help get rid of the monsters: Wonder Woman, the Incredible Hulk, Superman, whichever heroes your child is drawn to.

MESSY KIDS SPELL

Try to explain to your children, young and old, the benefits of being tidy and organised - how this can make them happier, more successful people.

For the littlies

Tell them about the 'tidy fairies'. Tidy fairies live in their room, and they can help your child and give them good luck if they're kept happy. They get very sad when where they live is really messy.

Make a special place for the tidy fairies. Buy a small colourful lamp and put it on a timer. Whenever the lamp comes on, the tidy fairies are 'in the house' and it's time for kids to clean up their rooms before the tidy fairies get too sad. When they finish, they can leave a little present at the base of the lamp - maybe a biscuit or flower. Then Mum and Dad can swap this for some pocket money or a little present.

For older kids

Buy older kids a lapis lazuli necklace and encourage them to wear it. Lapis cleanses the aura and encourages a more orderly approach to living. And maybe tidy fairies will work for them too!

SPELL TO MAKE A CHILD TELL THE TRUTH

Place a bay leaf on your child's tongue and they will be unable to lie. Bay encourages honesty and wisdom. It was sacred to the ancient priestesses of Apollo, who used to chew bay leaves before they had wise and prophetic visions.

SPELL FOR WHEN KIDS HEAD OFF TO SCHOOL FOR THE FIRST TIME

It's now been proved scientifically what witches/healers have known for ages - St John's wort helps to heal depression, both physically and magickally.

You will need

- Crystals (1 for each child)
- Dried St John's wort leaves
- Small amulet bags (1 for each child)

1. Place a crystal and 3 pinches St John's wort in a bag to make an amulet. Perhaps you could pack the amulet in the kid's lunch box or school bag, or they can keep it in their pocket to be close to the beneficial vibrations.

2. Before school, stand in a circle holding hands as you say:

   In the great circle of her creation,
   The goddess holds us in her protection.
   Her love is like the sun that warms and nourishes our hearts,
   Always merry meet and always merry part.

3. Throughout the day, know your child will be keeping their amulet bag close by and your love for each other will be felt happily all day.

FOR A CHILD HAVING PROBLEMS WITH ANOTHER CHILD AT SCHOOL

With a pen, write the troublesome child's name on a piece of paper and put it in an ice-cube tray with a garlic clove into which you've carved the child's name with a pin. Pour water over it and freeze. This will 'freeze' the actions of the child.

SPELL FOR MENTAL STRENGTH TO HELP DEAL WITH SCHOOL BULLIES

You will need

- A handful borage blossoms or leaves
- 1 teaspoon dragon's blood powder
- 1 teaspoon sandalwood powder
- Mortar and pestle (or a glass bowl and wooden spoon), for grinding and blending
- Piece of tiger's eye crystal
- Drop of blood or lock of hair from the person needing this spell
- Yellow silk pouch
- Red candle

1. Add the borage blossoms or leaves and dragon's blood and sandalwood powders to a mortar and pestle. Grind together and add the tiger's eye and drop of blood (or finely chop a small lock of their hair into the bowl).

2. Place the mixture in the yellow silk pouch and light the red candle. Holding the pouch in both hands, call on the archangel Michael:

   Archangel Michael, avail me of your mighty sword
   to cut down my oppressors and free me to be whole.

3. Have them carry the pouch at all times to ward off problems with bullies. Recharge its powers by lighting the red candle every night.

TO ENCOURAGE A CHILD TO DO THEIR HOMEWORK AND FIT INTO FAMILY LIFE

Encourage the child to keep snails as pets: snails encourage tenacity, patience and stability.

Together with your child, collect 3 empty snail shells from the garden. Crush the shells into a powder using a mortar and pestle and add 3 large pinches thyme (to encourage the removal of restlessness). Have the child sprinkle this around the base of an orange candle then light the candle as they say:

I can do my homework easily. I love being with my family.

They should repeat this three times then snuff the candle - don't blow it out because this will blow the spell's power away. Repeat this candle-lighting ritual morning and night for seven days.

FAMILY HEALING ALTAR

This spell is for when everyone in your house is sick and the bugs just won't go away! The altar will balance your home's elemental energies and encourage the healing attention of the goddess Hestia. You can make the altar on top of a table or chest of drawers.

- 2 blue candles
- 3 drops marjoram essential oil
- 3 drops thyme essential oil
- Oil burner
- Quartz crystal bowl
- Spring water
- Flower
- Photos of everyone looking well and happy
- Pin, for carving
- 1 thick red candle

1. Make an altar on top of a table or chest of drawers (or similar piece of furniture). Place the blue candles on the altar, then add the marjoram and thyme oils in the oil burner. Fill the bowl with spring water and place the flower in the water so it floats. Arrange photos of your family or household around the altar.

2. With a pin, carve an equal-armed cross shape into the red candle (to invoke the goddess Hestia). Place this in the centre of the altar.

3. After dinner, gather together around the altar, light the candles and oil burner, and all hold hands as one person (or everyone) recites:

   Hestia, goddess of home and hearth
   Make us healthy, make us laugh!

4. The key now is to laugh, either spontaneously or tell some jokes or funny stories - laughter is the best medicine and key to charging up this altar and sending healing energy through the home. Do this laughing ritual every night after dinner until the illness is gone. You can keep the oil burner topped up with oil and water throughout the day.

MOTHERS' DAY SPELL

You will need

- Pink, red and white carnations
- Parchment or paper
- Envelope
- Wax, for sealing
- Toothpick, for carving
- White candle

1. Make an altar somewhere your mother will see it when she awakes on Mothers' Day. Decorate a small table with pink, red and white carnations (sacred to mothers), which represent honour, love and respect.

2. Write a letter or poem to your mother on the parchment and put it in the envelope. Seal the envelope with wax and use the toothpick to write your initials in the wax. Carve your mother's name into the white candle. Place the sealed envelope and candle with the flowers on the altar and light the candle. Write a little note saying: 'Please read this letter and carry the candle with you to the dining room/kitchen when you're ready.'

3. Prepare a beautiful breakfast in honour of your mother. When she joins you, place the candle in the centre of the table and declare that the candle will burn all day as a symbol of your love and respect for your mother.

4. Your mother should keep some of the wax from the candle with the letter as a good-luck charm for the coming year.

Note: make sure your candle is a beautiful one, perhaps decorated and scented with oils. Also make sure it can burn safely (maybe in a glass holder).

TO HELP A MOTHER COMMUNICATE WITH HER TEENAGE DAUGHTER

You will need

- Feathers
- Lapis lazuli necklaces
- Yellow flowers
- Basil and rue

1. You and your daughter need to go out and find a feather each, then place it under each other's pillows. This will help to brush away resentful thoughts during sleep.

2. Go shopping together and buy each other a lapis lazuli necklace to wear at the throat to encourage clear and harmonious communication. You could put your necklaces on each other as you both say:

   With intent pure and whole, I will argue with you no more.

3. Arranging yellow flowers throughout the house will help, especially if you refresh them every Friday to benefit from the loving energy of Venus.

4. Add basil and rue to your family meals - these herbs reduce negativity and encourage harmony.

   Note: if you daughter is not keen to do any of these things, you can do them on your own - it will still help.

TO HELP EASE CONFLICT BETWEEN MOTHER AND DAUGHTER

Charge 2 pieces smoky quartz crystal by placing them at the base of a growing basil plant and leaving them overnight. In the morning, place each piece in a white pouch. The mother and daughter carries one each throughout the day - they will not be able to argue.

Smoky quartz helps to prevent arguments and encourages peace and harmony in conversations. Basil is a symbol of love and when grown in the kitchen and used in cooking it is calming for the nerves - medicinally and magickally.

SPELL TO MAKE THE IN-LAWS LIKE YOU

Pearls are featured in this spell because they encourage honesty, friendship and loyalty. Procure a mirror or photo frame inlaid with mother-of-pearl. Bewitch this gift by placing it in a box with 3 bay leaves and leave out under the light of a full moon. At midnight, tap the box three times with your left index finger and say:

> *I conjure by the moon's full light*
> *A charm of honour, free of spite.*
> *Love, harmony, I bestow on thee*
> *So shall those feel when they receive*
> *For the good of all.*
> *So mote it be.*

Leave the box out all night, then collect and give the gift to your new in-laws the next day.

TO IMPROVE COMMUNICATION WITH AN EX WHO IS REFUSING TO PAY ALIMONY

Do this spell on a Wednesday, for prosperity.

You WILL NEED

- Bergamot essential oil
- Picture of your ex
- Glass

1. With your index finger dipped in the oil, trace a heart over your ex's face then place the photo in your bra or top shirt pocket (close to your heart) before you meet them to discuss money.
2. If they speak unpleasant words or yell, catch their breath in a glass (hold the glass close to their face and cap your hand over the top as their breath falls in). Then run outside and release the air, asking the sun to nullify the negativity. This strange behaviour will have the added effect of breaking your ex's concentration and help to end the argument! Or maybe scare them enough that you are witch and they should treat you with respect!

DEATH OF A CHILD

To ease the grief and despair after a child passes, you can perform some gentle rituals. Violets bring comfort to those who have lost a child. Plant them on your child's grave or place a bunch in two vases, leaving one with your child and keeping the other at home where you can see them. The essence of the violets will ease your spirit and also your child's. Planting bluebells around your home can also offer peace.

CHILD BEREAVEMENT RITUAL

You will need

- Myrrh incense
- 1 white candle
- Photo of your child
- Violets

1. Burn myrrh incense — myrrh eases grief and helps you to understand the spiritual nature of life and death.

2. Light a white candle next to your child's photo and place some violets in a vase next to it. Take three deep breaths, gazing at the flame and ask the goddess for guidance in how to understand the loss of your child and move forward as they live forever in your heart. She will answer.

3. When she does, listen carefully and ask her any questions that come to you. Listen to the answers and check in with your body where you 'feel' the responses.

4. When you are ready, write down what resonated most powerfully. Read these words as often as you need to by the light of a white candle.

RITUAL FOR BEREAVEMENT

This is a ritual to honour the life of someone who has moved on to the next realm. It also helps those left behind to cope with their loss.

You will need

- Pieces of black paper
- Silver pen
- Crushed almonds
- Red ribbon
- Patchouli (dried leaves or powder)
- Myrrh resin
- Loving cup

1. Have everyone write a favourite memory of the deceased person on a black piece of paper with a silver pen. Place 3 pinches crushed almonds (to honour Hecate, goddess of the underworld) in the centre of each piece of paper, then fold and tie with a red ribbon.

2. Everyone then gathers by a lake, the ocean or any large body of water to work through their emotions.

3. Light a good-sized bonfire around which everyone stands in a circle. The person leading the ritual throws handfuls of patchouli and myrrh onto the fire and dedicates the ritual by saying:

    [Name], tonight we gather to share in love the sweet memory of your life and the eternity of your spirit.

4. Each person recites what they have written on their paper before throwing them in the fire. Then all join hands and repeat as one:

    Farewell dear friend, until we share, in another realm, our time again.
    Merry meet, merry part, merry meet again.

5. Pass around a loving cup filled with your loved departed one's favourite drink. When everyone has sipped from the cup, pour a little onto the fire and toast your dear one.

6. When you are ready, put out the fire and perhaps all go out together and share happy memories of your friend.

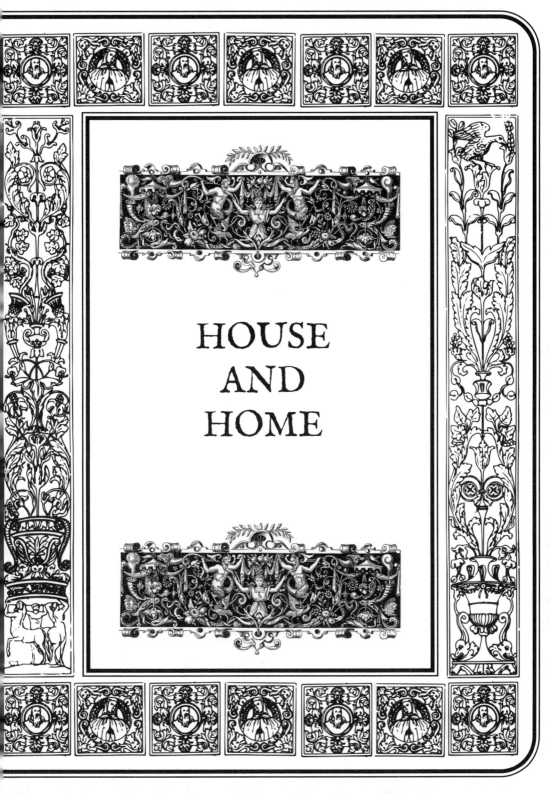

HOUSE
AND
HOME

PURIFY A HOUSE

Perform this powerful purification ritual before moving into a home that someone has lived in before.

You will need

- 1 white candle
- Bundle of dried sage
- Feather or fan
- Small bowl filled with salt water

1. To prepare the space, light the candle and place it in the centre of the room. This flame symbolises purity and illumination. Take a moment to ground yourself, feeling the energy of the earth beneath you and the sky above.

2. Ignite the bundle of sage and allow the smoke to fill the room. Visualise the smoke purifying the space, clearing away any stagnant or negative energy. Move clockwise around the room, gently waving the sage smoke with a feather or fan, focusing on areas that feel heavy or tense.

3. Dipping your fingers into the bowl of salt water, sprinkle it lightly around the room's perimeter. As you do so, envision a protective barrier forming, shielding the space from unwanted influences.

4. With clarity and purpose, declare your intentions for this space. Whether it be peace, love, creativity or abundance, infuse the room with your desires and aspirations. Visualise these intentions taking root and blossoming within the space.

5. Once you feel the energy has shifted and the space is cleansed, snuff the sage bundle and candle. Give thanks to the elements, spirits and energies that have assisted in this purification. Your home is now a sanctuary of light and positivity.

OLD ENGLISH RITUAL TO BLESS A HOME

In Old English times, people often blessed homes with rituals they believed would bring protection and prosperity to those who lived there.

YOU WILL NEED

- 6 white pillar candles (optional, if you don't have a hearth)
- Bowl of salt
- Piece of bread

1. Gather a group of people together, including the owners of the home and any family members or close friends who will be living there.

2. Light a fire in the hearth, which should be large enough to fill the room with warmth and light. If you don't have a hearth, light the candles on a tray and place on the kitchen table (the heart of the home).

3. Once the fire is burning brightly, everyone takes turns reciting a prayer or blessing in Old English. The prayer should ask for protection, prosperity and happiness for those who will be living in the home.

4. After everyone has spoken, take the bowl of salt and sprinkle it around the perimeter of the house, taking turns. If you are blessing an apartment, sprinkle the salt across the front doorstep and back doorstep if there is one. This will create a protective barrier around the home. Return to the hearth or candles in the kitchen.

5. Break the piece of bread into small pieces. Each person takes a piece and eats it, symbolising the sharing of blessings and good fortune.

With this ritual, the home is blessed with the protection and prosperity of the community. The owners can look forward to a happy and prosperous life in their new home.

TO CLEAR UP BAD LUCK AND ACCIDENTS AROUND THE HOUSE

You will need
- Dried spearmint
- Dried rosemary
- Dried thyme
- Sea salt
- Epsom salts

1. During the waxing moon, mix equal quantities of all the ingredients in a big bucket. As you do you this chant:

   Herbs of luck sublime
   Cleanse this home of mine.
   Good fortune bless this place
   so we dwell with happy face

2. In the morning before you go to work, sprinkle the mixture over the floors of the house. When you get home, sweep it all up (or vacuum with a brand-new bag). The herbs will have absorbed the negative energy, so take the mixture outside and burn it and then turn earth over it. Burning is important here - don't just bury it or throw in the bin.

TRIPLE FAST-ACTING JINX-REMOVING BATH AND FLOOR WASH

Borage is a magickal herb that enables you to feel happiness even in the most difficult of circumstances.

You will need

- 1 teaspoon camphor
- Infusion of borage (simmer a handful of leaves in 1 litre water for 20 minutes then strain)
- ½ bucket water
- Bible

Combine the camphor and borage infusion in the bucket of water, then use it to wash the floors, doors and windows. Put a cup of it in your bath. To add a touch of voodoo as you are bathing, read Psalm 23 from the Bible, focusing on releasing negativity in your environment.

SPELL TO PURIFY A HOUSE WHEN SAD OR DISTURBED ENERGIES REMAIN AFTER SOMEONE'S PASSING

YOU WILL NEED

- Frankincense incense
- White sage smudge sticks
- A witch's broom (use birch or twigs bound together - not plastic!)
- 1 pink candle
- Wreath of pink or white roses

1. Dress in white. Close all the windows and doors, then light the incense and smudge sticks and walk from room to room, fanning the smoke with your hand and intoning:

   Begone, begone to the past that dwells here.
   Begone, begone spirits and ghosts.
   It's time for you to move on away.
   Farewell, farewell, farewell.

2. When every room has been doused with smoke, open all the windows and doors then 'sweep' out the smoke with the broom. Don't let the broom touch the floor.

3. Once the air is clear, set up the candle surrounded by the wreath in the heart of the home (maybe the fireplace or where the sad energies are felt the strongest). Leave the candle burning all night in recognition of the spirits that have left - if they look back they'll know they don't need to return because their memory is honoured there.

4. In the morning, snuff the candle and bury it and the wreath under a tree.

SPELL TO GET RID OF UNWANTED GHOSTS OR ENTITIES IN YOUR HOUSE

You will need

- Frankincense incense
- 1 white candle
- Sacred book (either a witch's Book of Shadows, or the Bible, Quran, etc)
- Bell

1. In the room where the presence is, light the incense and candle then lay the book open with the bell and lit candle next to it.

2. State loudly and clearly:

   Move on and away, my demand is clear.
   Your presence is not welcome here.

3. Ring the bell, close the sacred book and snuff the candle flame with your fingers. Leave the incense burning until it is finished, then open the windows and let the smoke out.

To continue keeping the space clear, regularly burn frankincense incense. You can also make white linen sachets (sew up the sides of linen handkerchiefs), stuff with equal amounts of rosemary and garlic, and hang them around the room.

SIMPLE WALKING GHOST-REMOVAL SPELL

If you feel bothered by an unseen entity or presence in your home (or even a hotel room or Airbnb place where you're staying), you can perform a simple, respectful ghost-removal spell. Some people are more sensitive to entities than others, so if you travel frequently, you may want to take these supplies with you in a little kit and perform this spell when needed.

YOU WILL NEED

- White candle
- Small bottle of blessed extra-virgin olive or other vegetable oil (coconut is good)
- Candle holder
- Black cloth pouch or container of sea salt

1. Sit in the room where you feel the most energy - often the corner of a room. Visualise a sphere of white light around you for protection.

2. Dress (anoint) your candle with the oil by putting a drop of blessed oil on the index finger of your dominant hand and tracing it along the side of the candle. Place the candle in the holder and light it.

3. Using your non-dominant hand, take a handful of salt from the pouch. Holding the candle in your dominant hand, slowly walk backwards around the room sprinkling salt into each corner. If the space you're in has multiple rooms, walk backwards through each doorway and sprinkle a little salt across each threshold as well as the corners. As you walk chant:

    Spirit of the deceased, I offer you peace.
    Move on from this space, with sweet release.

4. When you have covered all the areas and the salt is gone, turn around and face forward. Snuff the flame with your fingers or blow out with intention, stating: 'I blow away all obstacles and negativity.'

HOW TO BLESS THE OIL

Holding the bottle to your heart, close your eyes and align yourself with the universal forces of peace. Visualise the crown of your head open with pale blue light streaming in and through you. When you feel relaxed and centred say:

May this oil be blessed with powers of peace
Sweetness and light, acceptance, release.

Open your eyes and sense the blue light swirling back into the cosmos.

TIPS TO SUBDUE OR GET RID OF A POLTERGEIST OR NEGATIVE SPIRIT ENERGY

Hang a wreath of garlic over the fireplace or mantle to repel the spirit. They often hang around hearths and chimneys (even when they're blocked up - walls don't stop spirits). Sprinkle salt over the front and back doorsteps.

Place whole raw eggs in the corners of the worst-affected rooms to absorb negative energy. After a week, bury them and replace with fresh ones if necessary.

Try talking to the spirit and respectfully asking it to leave. The negative ones are fuelled by fear and will manifest to the extreme that a living person's susceptibility allows it. So don't be scared - be respectful but don't put up with too much rubbish. Take firm action. You'll find a good purification ritual in my first book, *Witch: A Personal Journey*, which involves 'smoking out' negative energy and is very good for removing spirits. Australian Aboriginal people perform a similar ritual after a person dies to encourage their spirit to move on. They burn eucalyptus leaves (very smoky), filling the space with smoke then whisking it away, carrying the spirit with it.

Drinking mugwort tea (brew 2 teaspoons dried or ½ handful fresh mugwort in a pot of boiling water) can help to strengthen an individual's aura to be impervious to spirits (brew it half-strength for kiddies). Sweetened with a little honey, it's quite delicious and helps to aid a restful sleep.

SPELL FOR MOVING OUT FOR THE FIRST TIME

To enhance your good fortune, independence and safety, buy an Egyptian ankh necklace. The ankh is considered to be the 'key of life' and the perfect balance of feminine and masculine energies. Follow this trick to empower it before you wear it. Anoint yourself at your third eye, throat and heart chakras as well as the palms of the hands with frankincense essential oil. (Dilute with olive or jojoba oil if you have sensitive skin, though this oil is naturally soothing and anti-inflammatory.) Then put 1 drop frankincense oil at the point where the loop joins the stem of the ankh.

Hold the ankh in both hands towards the light of the full moon and then to your forehead as you say:

Gods of old, hold me safe as I venture from this space.

Every morning, hold the ankh and repeat this charm before you embark on your day. You can recharge the ankh's powers every full moon.

CHIPPY SPELL WHEN SELLING A HOUSE

Chip off a little of the front doorstep and wrap in a $20 note. Bury this in front of the doorstep or place under the doormat, so potential buyers have to step over it as they enter the house. It will help them think about buying.

CANDLE SPELL TO HELP SELL A HOUSE

Take a green candle and carve five notches in it with a pin. Anoint the notches with black pepper essential oil. Each night for five nights, burn the candle down to the next notch as you say:

Fire, speed my goal to me.
My house is sold easily.

By the sixth day someone will have made an offer.

SPELL TO HELP BUY A NEW HOUSE

To help when buying a new house, keep a round glass bowl with two gold-coloured goldfish. Fish encourage abundance and the fertility of good luck. This spell was originally designed for a person who wanted to buy the house they were currently renting. Keeping goldfish in the house would help that happen. If you're living in a house you are wanting to sell, keep two goldfish in a bowl near the front door - it will encourage buyers to be interested in the house.

TO SETTLE FROM YOUR OLD HOME INTO YOUR NEW HOME

YOU WILL NEED
- 3 sprigs fresh rosemary
- Gold ribbons
- Glass of berry juice (such as strawberry)
- White cloth

1. Make a doll with the rosemary sprigs and gold ribbon, tying them one over the other to resemble the torso, head, arms and legs.
2. Hang the doll in the kitchen until you move out. On the day of departure, break a little of the doll off and place in a glass of berry juice. Everyone who is relocating takes a sip from the glass and toasts the new home with words like: 'To our new home!' Then take down the doll and wrap in the white cloth.
3. Pour a little of the berry juice onto the front doorstep as you leave your old home for the last time.
4. When you arrive at your new home, hang the doll in the kitchen to bless and consecrate the space.

ANOTHER SPELL FOR MOVING

This spell is especially good if you have children.

You will need

- Blue cord (cut into 1-metre lengths)
- White pillowcase

1. Everyone takes a piece of blue cord. Holding their cords behind them, the family runs through the house, collecting up all the energy of the house. When the cords have absorbed all the 'home energy', everyone gathers in the kitchen to plait the cords together. Once the cords are woven into one magickal cord, place it on the floor and, holding hands, dance around it in a sunwise direction (clockwise in the northern hemisphere, anticlockwise in the southern hemisphere), chanting:

    We love our home,
    We love each other.
    We take with us
    Happiness and laughter.

2. Repeat the charm at least six times. When you are finished, everyone drop to the floor, place your hands on the cord and laugh as hard as you can!

3. Now the cord is charged and ready to take all the good things from your old home to your new home. Place it in a white pillowcase when you move. Once you arrive at your new home, hang it in the kitchen or over the front door for the first six weeks. Then if you like, you can return it to the pillowcase and store it or leave it hanging up!

SPELL TO MAKE SURE FRIEND HAS A SAFE JOURNEY AND EASE IN MOVING HOUSE

It's best to do this spell under a full or waxing moon as the night turns over from Wednesday to Thursday. Pluck a full five-fingered leaf of cinquefoil. Press and dry this herb between the pages of a book that you will give to your friend. (Maybe an affirmations book or even one of mine!) Give the book to your friend - as they carry it with them it will ensure a safe journey and move.

THE MAGICKAL GARDEN

Gardens have been considered holy and spiritual places for a long time - the original best-known garden is probably the Garden of Eden. Often our most profound spiritual experiences can occur in a pocket of nature.

- Make your garden magickal by studding the earth with crystals. A pond, fountain or bird bath can attract good fortune.
- If you have a problem with ants, don't kill them - ask them to leave. Do this during the waning moon over three successive nights. As you stand over the bustling ants, in a clear and firm voice say this ancient charm three times:

    Pismires, with blessings I greet thee
    Change your abode I sternly entreat thee!

- Spiders are considered lucky. An old wise woman's saying is: 'If you wish to live and thrive, let the spider run alive.'

TO GET RID OF POSSUMS

Make a witchy scarecrow to scare away possums. Dress it in white and red clothing and make the centre pole a willow branch (for purity and harmony). Around the base of the pole, stud the ground with quartz crystals. Stuff the scarecrow with thistle and sage (harmonising for animals) as you say:

Sage and thistle, from this place purge
The possum, the demon, the rogue, the scourge.

The possum has a right to live wherever it wants, so with this spell you are harmonising your wishes with it and encouraging it to make its home elsewhere.

CAT CHARMS

To calm a crazy cat:

- Grow the herb catnip. The smell is pleasant to cats, and they love to rub up against it and chew the leaves and twigs.
- Brew a weak infusion of red clover herbal tea and pour some over your cat's food to help calm your cat.
- Hold your cat often, consciously channelling calming, blue light over it.

TOP 5 HOUSEPLANTS TO PURIFY YOUR LIVING SPACE

Witches know that the ultimate magick comes from the heart of nature. Forging a strong bond with nature by nurturing houseplants is not only empowering, but it can sort out your health too!

The following houseplants all remove chemical vapours that build up in the home from paints, cleaning agents, solvents and other unhealthy chemicals - and they have magickal abilities too.

1. ARECA PALM (OR BUTTERFLY OR YELLOW PALM)	For peace and creativity
2. ENGLISH IVY	For protection and luck, especially good for newly weds
3. BOSTON FERN	To encourage psychic ability and intuition
4. PEACE LILY	To encourage harmonious energies and good communication
5. GERBERA DAISY	Great for encouraging happiness

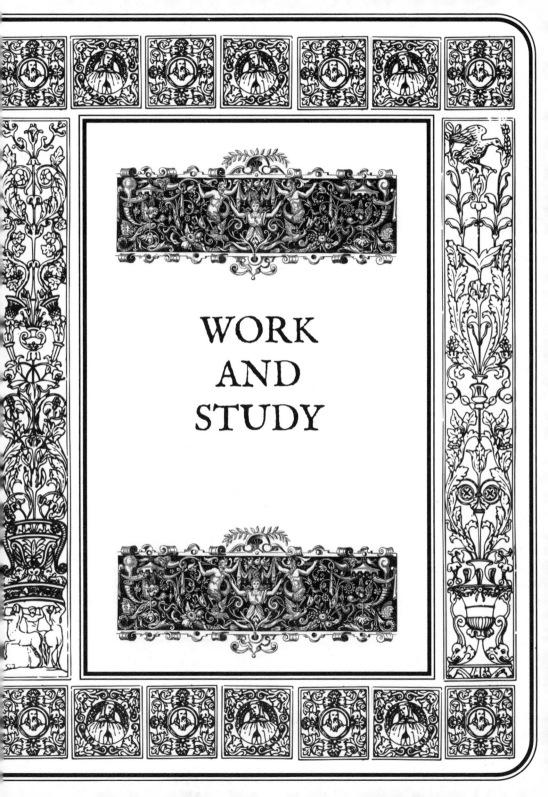

WORK
AND
STUDY

GOOD-LUCK SPELL FOR FINDING A NEW JOB OR INCREASING LUCK IN GENERAL

Pick a small bundle of twigs from a growing apple tree. (Ask the tree's permission and for its blessing before you do so.) Soak the twigs for a week in seawater, then dry and burn them on a hearth or small fire. Weave your hands through the smoke and say:

May luck continue in my hand and blossom like an apple bough.

Take the ashes of the fire and scatter them over the apple tree's roots as nourishment and a further boost to enhance your good fortune.

FOR A PERSON WONDERING IF THEY ARE IN THE RIGHT JOB

Three days before the full moon, with bare feet and in the morning sun, cut a sprig of sage with silver scissors. Tie the sage with a green ribbon and hang in the window of your bedroom. If it has not withered by the full moon, you are in the right job. If it has, you need to start investigating other options.

A SPELL TO HELP FIND A BETTER JOB

YOU WILL NEED

- White paper
- Green pen
- Garland of fresh ivy leaves
- 1 green candle
- 1 white candle
- 1 teaspoon honey
- 1 cup milk

1. Write a list on the white paper with the green pen, noting which of your talents you want to exploit and also what you want in a new job. Don't write the name of a job - just the aspects about it that appeal to you.

2. Place the paper on the ground under a growing tree and arrange a garland of ivy around it. Weave the ivy over and under itself and tie the ends together. Place the green and white candles in a cross shape on top. (Even unlit they carry the quality of fire, which will speed the process of this spell.) Stir the honey into the milk then pour the mixture over the candles as you say:

   Milk and honey,
   Pure and sweet.
   Fortify my dreams,
   Bring my goal to me.

3. Cover everything with fresh earth to allow your magickal plans to grow and take form in the material world.

TO HELP GET A PARTICULAR JOB

This spell is best performed on a Saturday.

You will need
- Piece of orange paper
- 1 orange candle

1. Write on the paper:
   This job is mine with harm to none
   For the good of all this spell is done.

2. Light the candle and meditate as you gaze at the flame. Visualise yourself working at your chosen place, conversing with colleagues, drinking water from the cooler, sitting at your desk. Try to involve all your senses - smell the air, hear the buzz of the place, and so on.

3. When you are ready and have a clear vision, chant the words you've written down three times. Fold the paper, place it under the candle and say: 'It is done.'

4. Leave the candle burning to keep charging the spell for as long as possible.

GOOD LUCK FOR A NEW SMALL BUSINESS

Perform this spell during the waxing moon.

You will need

- Cinnamon incense (for good luck)
- 2 green candles
- 1 large coin (like an Australian 50-cent piece, or similar in your local currency)
- 1 teaspoon alfalfa seeds (removes money worries)
- Peridot stone (encourages money to flow)
- Piece of green paper

1. Burn the cinnamon incense, light the candles, and place the coin, alfalfa seeds and peridot on the paper as you say:
   The moon does grow,
   And money does flow.

2. Fold the paper so everything is enclosed then repeat the charm three times, holding the package and feeling trust in the process and a sense of quickening of new business opportunities.

3. Put the folded paper into the top drawer of the desk where you do most of your work.

   Tip: bury coins by your front doorstep or place under the doormat to encourage money. Growing pots of mint around the office will help to ensure success.

TO GET AHEAD AT WORK

You will need

- Piece of green paper
- Plant pot
- Potting mix
- 1 fennel seedling (associated with wisdom)

1. On the paper, write your name, the type of job you do and the qualities you need to have to enhance your career.

2. Lick your thumb and trace over your name with your saliva. Fold up the paper, put in the pot then put the potting mix and seedling on top. As you do this say:

    Herb of wisdom grant to me
    The best at work so I succeed.

3. Nurture the plant - as it grows so will your career.

TO GET RID OF A CREEPY SLEAZY WORKMATE

You will need

- 1 teaspoon cayenne pepper
- 1 teaspoon crushed patchouli leaves
- 1 teaspoon powdered senna
- Tumbleweed
- ½ cup rice flour
- ¼ cup red paint powder

1. Grind and mix the herbs and tumbleweed, focusing on your desire to have this creep leave you alone.

2. Mix the flour and paint powder together then add the ground herb mixture as you say:

Be off away, be off and gone!
Dance down the road with thy creepy song.
Vanish as the winds of autumn dusk and twilight,
Begone from here, out of mind, out of sight!

3. Chant this over and over to magickally imprint the mixture with your intent.

Keep this mixture in a bottle and sprinkle a little around your desk or in the doorway of your office. Or even scatter some out the window, imagining him leaving you well alone.

SPELLS FOR WORK-RELATED STRESS

Lavender for multitasking

Grow a pot of lavender on your desk to keep on-the-job stress to a minimum. To increase its potency put red agate crystals around the base of the plant. This will help you work more effectively and handle multitasking better.

Invoke the goddess

Invoke Athena, the ancient Greek goddess of warriors and commerce by listening to flute music, eating olives and burning musk incense. She will look after you at work and give you strength and confidence.

Psychic shield

Create a psychic shield like Alexander the Great did when he went into the Valley of Diamonds to find treasure, which was guarded by snakes with the power to kill with a single glance. He overcame the serpents by ordering his soldiers to hold up their polished steel shields to repel the energy of the snake's gaze.

To do this at your workplace, place a mirror (a small makeup mirror or even a spare pair of glasses will do) on your desk, facing the doorway of your office or back over your shoulder, so people who stress you out don't approach you.

With your outstretched index finger, you can also trace a pentagram (the witch's sacred five-pointed star) over your desk or office doorway to stop people you don't like from entering.

BANISH POVERTY SPELL

Do this spell on a Wednesday.

You will need

- Knife, for carving
- 1 black candle
- 1 green candle
- Salt
- Candle holders
- Dried mint

1. Using the knife, cut into the base of the black candle to expose the wick. Carve into this candle the words 'poverty' and 'fear'.
2. Repeat the process with the green candle, this time carving the words 'wealth' and 'joy'.
3. Sprinkle a circle of salt. In the centre, place the black candle upside down in the holder and the green candle upright. Sprinkle the mint around the base of the green candle. Light both candles,

being aware that the inverted black candle is draining away and banishing poverty while the green candle is attracting wealth.

4. Say the following charm:

    The power of sacred fire is great.
    Bound to the flame I control my fate.

5. Focus on seeing yourself wealthy and successful and say three times:

    I banish fear and poverty.
    I welcome growth and money.

6. Seal the spell by saying: 'So mote it be.'

7. Leave the candles to burn. If you must go out, snuff then relight them when you come home. Once both are completely burned down, the spell is complete.

TO ENCOURAGE A SALE

Burn some alfalfa herb (not the sprouts) on a charcoal disc while you chant at least seven times:

   Money flows,
   Money grows.
   The sale is done,
   Money comes.

Save the ashes and put them in a green pouch. Carry the pouch with you to the sales meeting or auction you plan to attend.

TO BRING MONEY TO YOU

You will need

- Piece of green paper
- Pin, for carving
- 1 green candle
- Mint essential oil (or float 9 mint leaves in ½ cup olive oil)
- Candle holder

1. Write your financial goals on the paper. Be realistic: don't say you want to win the lottery; instead maybe say: 'I want to be valued more at my work so I will get a pay rise.' Or perhaps state an intention: 'I want to respect the money that comes into my life more so I am less frivolous with it.'

2. Using the pin, carve your name into one side of the candle and the word 'money' into the other. Anoint the candle with the mint oil, rubbing in well.

3. Fold the paper and place it under the candle holder. Light the candle and meditate on achieving your goals - see them happen in your mind. After a few minutes, snuff the candle. Relight it every night for seven nights or until the candle is gone. Your money situation will improve.

DOMINATION SPELL

Here is a spell to vanquish your competitors!

You will need

- Paintbrush
- Black paint
- Pottery bowl
- Broomstick

1. Using the paintbrush, paint the names of your competitors in black paint on the bowl.

2. Take it to a crossroads near you. Holding it above your head, call on Hecate, the great witches' goddess.

   Hecate, avail me of your might
   That I shall win in everyone's sight!
   This I ask with harm to none
   But I get in first and MY will is done!

3. Smash the bowl and sweep away the remnants in the four directions with your broomstick. Then bow to Hecate in gratitude and walk away without looking back.

TO FIX MONEY PROBLEMS

You will need

- 3 almonds
- Crystal glass
- 3 drops bergamot essential oil
- Green velvet pouch

1. At sunrise on a Wednesday morning, place the almonds in the glass. Facing the sun as it comes over the horizon, drip a drop of oil on each almond and say:

   By one, money comes.
   By two, this is true.
   By three, so mote it be.

2. Put the almonds in the green pouch and hold it out in the palm of your right hand to absorb the sun's regenerative and strengthening powers. Keep the pouch with you for 21 days and your money situation will improve.

SEND NEGATIVE ENERGY BACK TO FINANCE COMPANIES

You will need

- Red pen
- Envelope
- Black feather
- Stamp

Using the red pen, address the envelope to the offending party. Do not write a return address. Take the horrible letter or document you've received and burn it, making sure you save the ashes. Recite this chant:

> *Your insult is no harm to me.*
> *What you project returns in three.*
> *What you say is not right.*
> *I fling it back with all my might.*

THOTH'S BLESSING

In ancient Egypt, Thoth (the god of writing, knowledge and wisdom) was revered as the divine scribe and mediator. He played a crucial role in maintaining the universe's balance and was associated with the moon, which he used to measure time. Thoth was often depicted with the head of an African Ibis (a bird sacred to him), symbolising his connection to intellectual pursuits and scholarly endeavours. The patron of scribes and scholars, Thoth was believed to have invented writing and language, and as such was a powerful figure in the realms of knowledge and learning.

This spell asks for Thoth's blessings to help you study. Find a quiet space where you won't be disturbed and do this spell when the moon is high in the sky.

You will need

- Small statue or image of Thoth (optional but beneficial)
- 1 blue or white candle (symbolising knowledge and wisdom)
- Piece of paper

1. Place the statue of Thoth in front of you, if you have one. Light the candle and place it next to Thoth. Take a few deep breaths to centre yourself and clear your mind.

2. Ask for Thoth's blessings. Hold your hands over the candle and say:

   Great Thoth, Lord of wisdom and writing,
   Scribe of the gods, master of knowledge,
   I humbly ask you on this moonlit night
   To lend me your strength and divine insight.

3. On the piece of paper, write down your specific request. For example:

   Thoth, guide me in my studies,
   Grant me clarity of mind and sharpness of memory,
   Let my efforts be fruitful and my knowledge grow,
   So I may pass my exams and use my wisdom for the greater good.

4. Hold the paper close to your heart and visualise yourself studying effectively, understanding the material and successfully passing your exams. See yourself in the future, using your knowledge and credentials to make a positive impact in the world. If you can focus on your study efforts as contributing to the world and not just for your personal gain, universal forces will work in your favour to aid you in your endeavours.

5. Place the paper under the candle or in front of Thoth, and say:

   Thoth, accept this humble request,
   As I seek to honour you through my quest.
   Let my studies be blessed with your light,
   And my mind be as sharp as my future is bright.

6. Spend a few moments in silent meditation, focusing on your intention and feeling gratitude for Thoth's guidance and support. Visualise his presence filling you with wisdom and knowledge. Note any messages or tips for study that may present in your mind as you meditate.

7. When you feel ready, close the spell by saying:

Great Thoth, I thank you for your aid,
And for the knowledge I will gain.
With your wisdom, I now proceed
To fulfil my goals and succeed.

8. Extinguish the candle and keep the paper with your study materials as a reminder of your intention and the support you've invoked.

Note: make sure you follow through with your studies, trusting that Thoth's guidance is with you. Revisit this spell whenever you need additional support or a confidence boost.

RITUAL FOR EXAM SUCCESS INSPIRED BY SETNE AND THE *BOOK OF THOTH*

When the ancient Egyptian magician Setne wanted to memorise the *Book of Thoth*, an age-old text of magical knowledge, he employed a powerful method. He transcribed the entire book onto fresh papyrus. He then soaked the papyrus in beer (which people more commonly drank than water in those times) until it dissolved with the letters disappearing into the water. He drank this mixture. This ritual allowed him to internalise the book's contents, learning every word by heart.

You can adapt this process to help remember important points for your exams. Here's how:

- 1 blue or white candle (symbolising knowledge and wisdom)
- Piece of paper
- Non-toxic water soluble pen
- Bowl
- Beer or water (as a non-alcoholic alternative)

1. Set up a quiet study space where you won't be disturbed. Carve your initials into the candle then light it, placing it on your writing surface (desk or table).

2. On the paper, write down the key points you need to remember for your exam. This could be important facts, formulas or summaries of crucial concepts.

3. Place the paper with your notes in the bowl. Pour the beer or water over it and let the paper dissolve into the liquid, stirring gently.

4. When the paper has dissolved, drink the liquid. As you drink, visualise the information being absorbed into your mind. Feel the clarity and sharpness of memory taking root within you. Visualise yourself during the exam, confidently recalling and writing down the answers.

5. When you feel ready, extinguish the candle to close the spell.

Continue your studies with the confidence that Thoth's wisdom and the ritual's power are aiding your memory and understanding. Repeat this ritual if you need a boost or have additional study material you want to imbibe.

SPELL FOR EXAM SUCCESS AND ACCELERATED LEARNING

To perform this spell, you need to find a quiet space in nature where there is bare earth and you can concentrate.

YOU WILL NEED

- Quartz crystal
- Bowl of salt water

1. Cleanse, consecrate and empower the quartz crystal with your intention. Wash the crystal in the bowl of salt water. Then lick your thumb and trace your initials on the crystal in your saliva while focusing on your desire to enjoy studying and successfully pass your exams or tests.

2. Holding the quartz crystal in the hand you write with, trace a symbol into the earth that represents your need. This could be a symbol for knowledge that you invent or something that resonates with your intention. As you trace the symbol, visualise yourself studying, concentrating and focusing. See yourself having already passed the exam or mastered the new skill you're to be tested on. Feel the confidence and relief of success wash over you like getting into a warm bath. Sense how the earth is anchoring your mental goals into physical reality.

3. Hold the quartz crystal in both hands and touch it to you forehead as you say:

   With this crystal, I focus and see,
   My mind is sharp, my thoughts are free.
   Success in tests comes easily
   As is my will so must it be.

4. Spend a few more moments in silent meditation, focusing on your intention and feeling gratitude for the guidance and support you are receiving. Visualise wisdom and knowledge

filling you. When you are ready, trace your initials in the earth with your index finger in gratitude to Mother Earth for holding space and helping you manifest your intention. Always keep your quartz crystal with you as you study and are being tested.

Note: make sure you follow through with your studies and test preparations, trusting that the energy and intention you've set will give you a boost to bring you success.

CRYSTALS FOR STUDYING AND LEARNING

BLOODSTONE	Bloodstone can remove mental and physical blocks, promoting clarity and rejuvenation.
FALCON'S EYE (BLUE TIGER'S EYE)	Falcon's eye enhances focus and clarity, making it easier to concentrate on tasks.
FLUORITE	Fluorite can strengthen analytical and intellectual abilities, aiding in decision-making and concentration.
RHODOCHROSITE	An energy-giving stone, rhodochrosite helps to maintain motivation and stamina, perfect for long study sessions.
SMOKY QUARTZ	An energiser, smoky quartz dispels negativity and promotes grounding and stability.
SODALITE	A stress-reducer, sodalite promotes emotional balance and calmness, ideal for reducing exam anxiety.
SUNSTONE	An energiser, sunstone boosts vitality and promotes a positive mindset.
TURQUOISE	Turquoise aids in verbal communication, making it easier to articulate thoughts and ideas.

HOW TO USE THE CRYSTALS

JEWELLERY	Wearing crystals as jewellery (necklaces, rings, bracelets, earrings) keeps them close to your body, so their energy is with you throughout the day. The jewellery design can also enhance a crystal's power, such as setting a turquoise or bloodstone in an ankh for energy, suspending an amethyst in a pentagram for balance or embedding a clear quartz in a spiral for inspiration.
POCKETS OR POUCHES	Carrying small stones in a pocket or small pouch lets you discretely keep their energy close. Thumbing stones in a pouch with your fingers can be good for stress relief.
STUDY AREA	Placing crystals on your desk or in your study area helps to support your learning and focus.

HELP FOR EXAMS

YOU WILL NEED
- Rosemary essential oil
- Piece of citrine quartz
- Piece of clear quartz

1. Burn 5 drops rosemary oil in water on the oil burner. Holding the citrine in your right hand and clear quartz in your left, inhale the scent of rosemary and say:

   My mind is clear, my knowledge good.
   Success is mine, be as it should.

2. Before your exam, place a drop of rosemary oil on your temples and place the crystals on the desk while you do your exam.

IDEAS TO HELP SUCCESSFUL STUDYING AND EXAMS

When you are studying, burn 5 drops rosemary and 2 drops lemon essential oils in an oil burner to help mental clarity and your recall of facts and figures. Keep a piece of citrine quartz with you when studying and doing exams to help your logical and creative mental efficiency!

THE ONLINE
WORLD

PROTECTION SPELL FOR
SOCIAL MEDIA ACTIVITY

You WILL NEED

- 1 white candle
- Clear quartz crystal or another protective crystal you resonate with
- Small bowl of salt
- Lavender or sage incense (for purification)
- Feather
- Piece of paper
- Fireproof bowl

1. Find a quiet and comfortable space where you won't be disturbed. Set up your altar or sacred space with the white candle, quartz crystal, bowl of salt and incense.

2. Light the incense and using the feather or your left hand, fan the smoke around you and over your smart device or computer to purify the space and your energy.

3. Taking the bowl of salt, walk around the perimeter of your space in a sunwise direction (clockwise in the northern hemisphere, anticlockwise in the southern hemisphere), sprinkling a small amount of salt as you go. Visualise a protective circle forming around you, shielding you from negativity.

4. Sit in the centre of your circle, close your eyes and take a few deep breaths to centre yourself. Visualise roots extending from the soles of your feet into the earth, grounding you in its protective energy and allowing positive authentic online interactions to occur.

5. Light the white candle, which symbolises purity and protection. Hold the crystal in your hands and say:

    By the light of this candle and the power of this crystal,
    I call upon the guardians of light to protect me from harm.

> *May positivity and love surround me as I navigate the realms of social media.*

6. Take the piece of paper and write down your intentions for using social media in a positive and empowering way. Be specific about the type of energy you wish to attract and interactions you seek.

7. Holding the paper in your hands, again visualise yourself surrounded by a bubble of protective light. Say aloud or in your mind:

> *With this spell, I ward off negativity and invite positivity,*
> *May my interactions on social media be filled with kindness and understanding.*
> *As I engage online, I am protected, empowered and uplifted.*

8. Place the paper near the candle and allow it to catch fire, visualising your intentions being released into the universe. Let the paper burn safely in a fireproof bowl until it turns to ash.

9. Thank the guardians and energies who have aided you in this spell. Close the circle by walking widdershins (anticlockwise in the northern hemisphere, clockwise in the southern hemisphere) around the perimeter, envisioning the protective energy retracting back into the earth. Snuff out the candle, sealing the spell.

Continued practice

Keep the crystal on your desk or near your computer as a reminder of your protection spell. Whenever you feel the need for extra protection or positivity while using social media, you can repeat this spell or simply visualise the protective bubble around you.

Remember, the power of this spell lies in your intentions and belief in your actions. Trust its effectiveness and know you are always surrounded by positive energy and protection when engaging in the online world.

GET RID OF AN ADDICTION
TO THE INTERNET

Burn frankincense incense. Tie black ribbons around each wrist and sprinkle a mixture of cayenne pepper and dried ginger around your computer in a sunwise direction (clockwise in the northern hemisphere, anticlockwise in the southern hemisphere) as you say:

> *I bind myself from this affliction.*
> *I am free with no addiction.*
> *I release the internet*
> *So that my time is better spent.*

Do this ritual starting on a Saturday and repeat every morning until the following Saturday.

CEREMONY FOR BLESSING
ONLINE ACTIVITIES

This ritual invokes ancient deities and blesses all your online activities, including posting on social media, dating and even sending emails. It is best performed on a Wednesday (Mercury's day, associated with communication and presence).

You will need

- Multicoloured altar cloth (representing diversity and creativity)
- 1 yellow candle (for communication and clarity)
- 1 blue candle (for wisdom and truth)
- 1 green candle (for growth and harmony)
- Incense (such as sandalwood or frankincense for spiritual insight and purification)
- Images or symbols of the goddesses Saraswati and Athena, and the god Thoth (honouring diverse cultural origins)

1. Find a quiet, sacred space where you won't be disturbed. Set up your altar with the cloth, candles, incense and images of the deities. Light the incense and take several deep breaths, centring yourself to connect with the divine presences.

2. Light the yellow candle and say:

   I honour Saraswati, goddess of wisdom and communication from the Indian tradition.
   Bless my words, guide my expression
   With clarity and grace in every interaction.

3. Light the blue candle and say:

   I honour Athena, goddess of wisdom and strategy from the Greek tradition.
   Bless my mind, guide my thoughts
   With truth and insight in all I share.

4. Light the green candle and say:

   I honour Thoth, god of wisdom and writing from the Egyptian tradition.
   Bless my messages, guide my hand
   With wisdom and harmony, let my words stand.

5. Gaze at the images of the god and goddesses, noting any messages and advice that come through - or any feelings that present in your body. When you feel it is time, thank the divinities:

   With gratitude and grace, I seal this rite,
   My online presence, shining bright.
   As I will, so mote it be,
   Blessed and empowered, I am free.

6. Thank Saraswati, Athena and Thoth for their guidance and blessings. Allow the candles to burn down completely if safe to do so, or snuff them out with gratitude.

RITUAL FOR ONLINE DATING PROTECTION AND EMPOWERMENT

This ritual is to protect yourself from negative experiences while online dating and attract a meaningful, exciting and loving relationship. Perform it on a Monday for lunar alignment.

You will need

- Sage bundle (for cleansing)
- 1 black candle (for protection)
- Amethyst crystal (for protection and clarity)
- 1 blue candle (for wisdom and communication)
- Lapis lazuli crystal (for wisdom and truth)
- Bay leaves (for protection and success)
- Lavender flowers (for peace and attracting love)
- Sea salt
- White pouch
- Small mirror

1. Arrange the ritual items on your altar. Light the sage bundle and move it around your body and space, cleansing any negative energy. Say:

   Sacred smoke, cleanse and protect,
   Clear the energy, let no harm infect.
   Only positive energy comes online
   So I have love that never lies.

2. For online protection, light the black candle and hold the amethyst crystal in your dominant hand. Say:

   Black flame of night, protect and guard.
   Amethyst crystal, shield me
   From deceit and harm, free me.
   Only truth and love shall find me.

3. For harmonious communication, light the blue candle and hold the lapis lazuli crystal in your non-dominant hand. Say:

> *Flame of wisdom, clear and bright,*
> *Lapis lazuli, reveal truth by sight.*
> *Guide my words and actions to be wise and true,*
> *Attracting love that's sincere and pure.*

4. Place the bay, lavender and sea salt in the pouch. Crush them together as you look at yourself in the mirror and chant:

> *By the power within and all around,*
> *Confidence and love in me abound.*
> *With this bundle, I attract and see*
> *A love that's true and meant to be.*

5. Keep the amethyst and lapis lazuli with you or place them near your online dating space to continue attracting protective and wise energy. When online, crush the pouch to charge the spell to protect again.

MEDITATION RITUAL FOR HEALING SUPERFICIALITY IN ONLINE DATING

You will need

- Comfortable meditation cushion or chair
- Sandalwood or frankincense incense (for spiritual insight and purification)
- Rose quartz crystal (for self-love and attracting genuine love)
- Amethyst crystal (for spiritual clarity and transformation)

1. Set up a quiet, peaceful space with the meditation cushion and ritual items. Light the incense, close your eyes and take several deep breaths, allowing the sacred scent to bless you.

2. Hold the rose quartz in your left and amethyst in your right hand. Reflect on your desire to move beyond superficial interactions

and attract meaningful, genuine connections. Feel the energy of the crystals merging with your intentions.

3. Drop into meditation with your back straight and hands resting gently on your knees, palms up, still holding the crystals. Focus on the light playing behind your eyelids as you breathe deeply, inhaling through your nose and exhaling slowly through your mouth.

4. Imagine a soft, pink light glowing in your heart centre. With each breath, see this light growing brighter and expanding outwards, filling your body with warmth and love. Visualise it extending beyond your physical body, creating a protective and loving aura around you.

5. Now visualise yourself engaging in sincere, heart-centred conversations with potential partners - interactions filled with honesty, respect and genuine interest. See the person looking at your online profile, taking time to explore and making a conscious choice to contact you.

6. Repeat mantras to yourself (memorise these beforehand):

    I attract genuine, meaningful connections.
    I am worthy of deep and authentic love.
    I release superficiality and embrace true connections.

7. Stay meditating for as long as feels good.

Repeat this meditation daily or weekly to reinforce your intentions and maintain a heart-centred approach to online dating. Keep the rose quartz and amethyst near you during your online dating activities to stay connected to the healing and deeper connections this ritual offers.

OUTDOOR RITUAL FOR GAMERS

This ritual blesses gamers with stamina and fortitude for long hours of play, and creates a bridge for transitioning back into everyday life, ensuring a healthy balance between the physical and virtual worlds. It is best performed in the early morning or late afternoon, preferably on a weekend when you have plenty of time to connect with nature.

You will need

- Portable altar (a small cloth or blanket)
- Small bowl of spring water (for cleansing and renewal)
- 1 red candle (for stamina and energy)
- Citrine crystal (for energy and motivation)
- 1 green candle (for grounding and balance)
- Haematite crystal (for grounding and protection)
- Sprig of pine or cedar (for resilience and strength)
- Cedar or sandalwood incense (for grounding and protection)
- Small snack of nuts or fruit (symbolising physical nourishment)

1. Find a quiet outdoor space - such as a park, forest clearing or garden - where you can sit comfortably on the ground surrounded by nature and won't be disturbed. (And be fire safe! Don't light candles in the bush on a hot, dry day.)

2. Arrange the ritual items on the altar. Sprinkle some spring water around your space to contain the energies for your magick.

3. Light the red candle and hold the citrine in your hand. Feel its energy and warmth as you say:

   I summon stamina and energy.

4. Light the green candle and hold the haematite in your hand. Feel its grounding and stabilising energy as you say:

   I embrace grounding and balance.

5. Take the pine sprig and hold it up to the sky. Feel the resilience and strength of nature flowing through you as you say:

   I am resilient and strong.

6. Dip your fingers in the bowl of spring water and sprinkle it lightly over your head and hands. Feel the cleansing and renewal as you say:

   I am cleansed and renewed.

7. Take the snack from your altar and eat it mindfully, savouring each bite. Feel it grounding you and nourishing your body as you say:

   I am grounded and nourished.

8. Stay in this space and look around you. Observe all the beauty of the natural world - the sun on the leaves, birds and insects, colourful flowers, clouds moving across the sky - note everything you see by saying it aloud.

9. When you are ready, thank Mother Earth for holding space for you. Extinguish the candles safely and pack up your altar. Leave only footprints behind.

ONGOING ONLINE GAMING HEALTH

Perform this ritual once a week to maintain stamina, balance and a healthy connection between your virtual and physical lives.

Keep the citrine and haematite near your gaming setup to remind you of your connection to nature.

Regularly spend time outdoors to ground yourself and reconnect with nature, balancing the hours you've spent online.

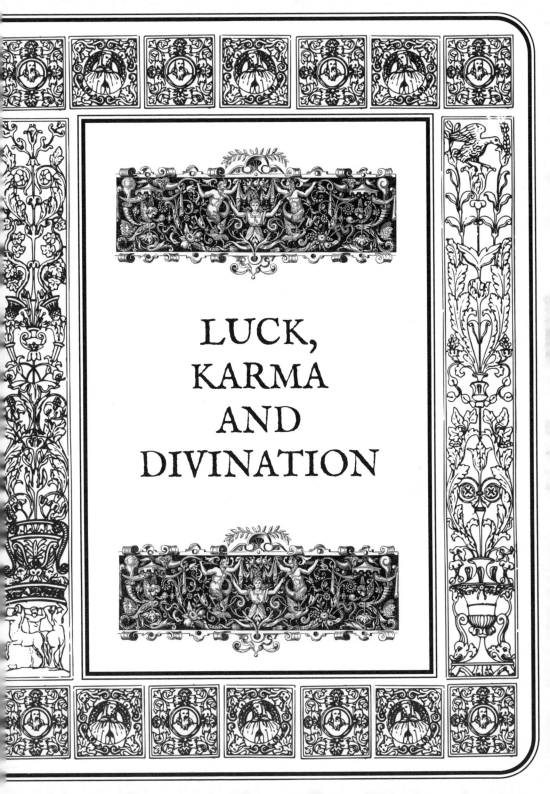

LUCK,
KARMA
AND
DIVINATION

SPELL TO ENSURE GOOD LUCK

Make a fire outside and throw on 7 big handfuls eucalyptus leaves and 7 big handfuls dried chamomile. Do not light the fire yet. Then have a cold shower and go outside skyclad (naked). Light the fire and leap through the smoke seven times as you say:

Away, away,
Bad luck and woe.
The tide is turned
My fortune grows.

When the fire dies down, turn the ashes into the soil to bury your old bad luck.

SPELL FOR DIRECTION AND HINTS FOR ENCOURAGING GOOD LUCK

This is a good spell to do if you are wondering if you should change jobs or life's direction. For example, if you drive an Uber for a living but have been having a lot of accidents (not your fault) and challenges, you may be wondering if you should still drive an Uber or do something else.

YOU WILL NEED
- Sea salt
- 1 white candle
- Handful fennel seeds
- Sprig of dill

1. Sprinkle a large, flat, even circle of sea salt (use powder not crystals). With the index finger of your right hand, trace a line evenly down the centre to divide the circle in half. To the left of the line, the answer is 'yes' and to the right, 'no'.

2. Light the white candle to help focus your mind and draw on the illuminating powers of fire.

3. Stand over the circle and hold a handful of fennel seeds in your right hand. (Fennel is a herb of wisdom and using the seeds will prevent you from re-asking the question ... otherwise how are you going to pick them out of all the salt?! You will get the right answer straight up.)

4. Before you drop the seeds, into the circle say:

   Herb of wisdom,
   Herb of insight,
   Give me the answer
   That is right.

5. Ask your question out loud (in this case: 'Should I continue being an Uber driver?') Close your eyes and drop the seeds - where the majority of them fall will indicate your answer.

6. To encourage better luck, hang a sprig of dill from the rear-vision mirror, and keep the car clean and windows open as much as you can to prevent stagnant energy building up. You can also trace (with your right index finger) the pentagram (five-pointed star) onto the driver's door and front of your car for protection.

TO REVERSE BAD KARMA

You can do this spell on the first night of the waning moon (after a full moon). Do it in the evening by the ocean or a large body of water. As the sun sets, so your bad fortune will drain away.

1. Hold a stone or object that you feel is appropriate. Project your hang-ups, tears and shame into it. Focus on letting all your emotions flow into the rock. When you have done this say:

I release the past.
I release my fears.
I let go of all that harms
My future is clear
My life is charmed.

2. Throw the rock into the water, preferably as the sun drops below the horizon. Be conscious of its fading light taking away your bad fortune. Repeat this spell for seven nights for really difficult situations.

SPELL TO DISPERSE NEGATIVE INFLUENCES

You will need

- 1 broom
- 2 white candles
- 2 black candles
- Sandalwood incense
- 3 drops pennyroyal essential oil
- Bowl of spring water
- 1 sprig rue
- Piece of paper

1. Sweep the air with the broom to clear the energy before you do the spell.

2. Set up white candles in the north and east, and black candles in the south and west. Light the incense and candles and sit in the centre. Inhale deeply and relax.

3. Add the pennyroyal oil to the bowl of water then dip the rue into it and splash yourself saying:

Bad luck [or whatever you wish to get rid of] be gone!

4. Repeat this at least nine times, then write on the paper what you want to let go of. Draw a big cross over it and burn it in the flame of the black south candle. Bury the ashes.

'GO AWAY' SPELL

If someone is bothering you, try rubbing them out. As they walk towards you, imagine a giant eraser deleting them or maybe visualise them disappearing under a flood of liquid paper. Visualisation is the key to a lot of magick, so even though this seems funny, hold your vision and focus. If you can do this spell during the waning moon, it can further help you remove things from your life that no longer serve you or irritate you.

As you practise this spell, you will find that the person will gradually stop bothering and approaching you - and also that you'll feel less irritated if you have to be around them for any reason.

THE BIG FREEZE

You can double up on the 'go away' spell by doing the 'big freeze'. Write the person's name on a piece of paper, put it in an ice-cube tray, pour water over it and freeze in the freezer. If you must associate with the person (for work or whatever), maybe it's just one aspect of their behaviour that bugs you. In that case, next to their name write the action and freeze that to be more specific.

TO MAKE A DECISION

Make a flat circle of salt. With your forefinger, trace 'yes' on the left-hand side and 'no' on the right. Hold a pendulum (which you can buy from a new-age store or make yourself by tying a leather thong or cord around a nugget of crystal - citrine is good) in the centre of the circle and the pendulum will begin to arc towards the better choice.

INCENSE DIVINATION

Burn powdered incense on self-igniting charcoal (light by holding the charcoal with tweezers or tongs) or place 3 sticks incense upright and close together.

Watch the smoke carefully and ask a question:

- Smoke twisting to the right means 'yes'.
- Smoke twisting to the left means 'no'.

If you are burning incense on a charcoal disc, try dropping fennel seeds onto it - they explode in the heat:

- One pop means 'yes'.
- Two pops mean 'no'.
- If there is silence the outcome is unclear.
- If the smoke drifts towards you it's a positive omen.

Good incense to use for divination include:

- a blend of damiana and mugwort herbs
- patchouli, cinnamon, frankincense, nutmeg and fennel.

Other uses for incense:

DIETING	A sweet scent can lessen cravings for excess food. Try honey and spice blends, also myrrh, amber and rose.
TO RELIEVE DEPRESSION	Lavender, mandarin
APHRODISIAC	Strawberry, sandalwood, musk and aloe

DIVINATION TO SEE IF A HUSBAND OR LOVER HAS BEEN UNFAITHFUL

YOU WILL NEED

- White sand
- Piece of clear quartz crystal
- Piece of string about 30 cm (12 inches) long
- 1 fern branch

1. Make a large circle with the white sand. Tie the quartz crystal to one end of the string.

2. Trace the fern through the sand to imbue the area with the power to see truth. With your index finger in a sunwise direction (clockwise in the northern hemisphere, anticlockwise in the southern hemisphere), trace a large circle in the sand with a line down the middle - to the left is 'yes', to the right is 'no'.

3. Tie the other end of the string to the index finger you traced the sand with. Hold out your finger over the line with the crystal dangling. Focus on your question: 'Has my lover been unfaithful?' See which way the crystal starts to swing - that will be your answer.

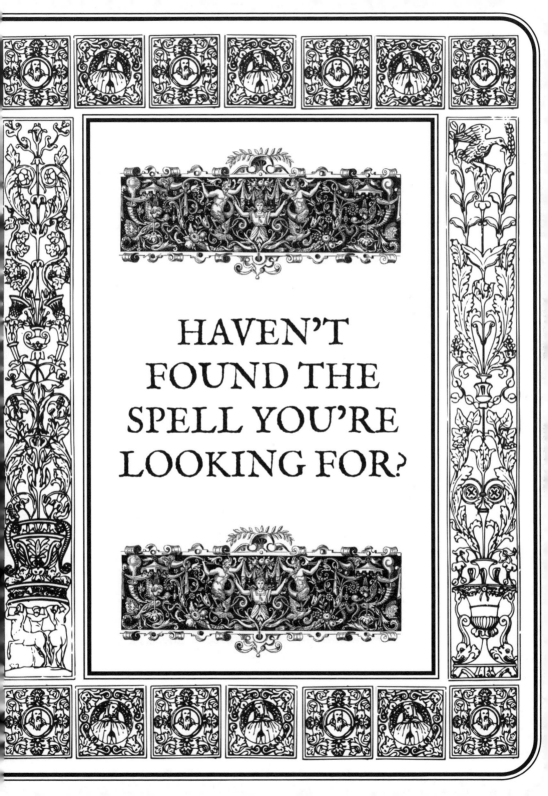

HAVEN'T FOUND THE SPELL YOU'RE LOOKING FOR?

Look in here for one-off and uncategorised spells. You might not find exactly what you're looking for but may discover something else that tickles your fancy.

BIRTHDAY RITUAL

Rather than putting candles on a birthday cake, invite your guests to each bring a candle into which they have carved their name and their wish for the birthday girl or boy. Set up the candles around the cake. Instead of blowing out the candles, the birthday person lights them as everyone sings 'Happy Birthday'. Keep the candles burning throughout the party to bring everyone's good wishes into the birthday person's life.

CHINESE NEW YEAR RESOLUTIONS SPELL

Chinese New Year is an opportunity to connect with ancient energies and make big changes that can positively affect your life for years to come. This spell is for people who stuffed up their 1 January resolutions - here's a second chance!

You will need

- Pink paper (the Chinese colour of good luck and good fortune)
- Stick of wood 30 cm long (one of the five sacred Chinese elements, along with metal, soil, water and fire)
- Pink ribbon

Write your resolutions or goals on the paper and roll around the stick. Wrap the ribbon around the paper and stick, spiralling it like a DNA strand and tying at both ends. Create as many of these resolution sticks as you like. The more you create, the more you'll enforce your goals. Stand them in a vase or other holder somewhere you can see them every day.

WEDNESDAY SPELL FOR CONJURING MERCURY AND HAVING YOUR WISH GRANTED

Mercury is the planetary ruler of Wednesday. He is seen as a guide between the worlds. Witches can work with Mercury to link the material plane of earth with the astral plane. To perform this spell, you'll need access to a crossroads with privacy to dig a hole (or a point where three or four paths meet in the forest, bush or somewhere private).

The herb Job's tears is a testament to humility and resilience. The seeds symbolise Job's unwavering faith amidst his trials. Legend holds that his tears, a manifestation of the suffering he endured, enriched the very soil beneath him and grew nourished by his refusal to yield to despair.) Important: the wish you have needs to be expressed in nine words exactly.

You will need
- Black poppy seeds
- Dried oregano
- 2 white candles
- Charcoal disc
- 9 black beans or seeds of Job's tears
- Chalice (or stemmed glass) with spring water

1. Grind the poppy seeds and oregano together to make incense.

2. Light the candles, burn the incense on the charcoal disc and stamp the earth three times to get the attention of the other worlds where parallel universes exist, including the reality your wish lives in. You are asking the spirits that exist between the worlds to help weave your wish into a reality that manifests in your world.

3. Say this incantation solemnly:

Spirit of air,
Guide of the dead,
Hear my words as they are said.
Mighty ones, pay heed to me.
Grant my wish,
So mote it be.

4. Spread the beans in a row. Whisper one word of your wish to each one. Sprinkle them with water from the chalice, then take them in your hand and pass them through the smoke of the incense.

5. Bury the beans at the crossroads. When you have covered them, place your hand over the spot and say:

   My gratitude to those who rule the realms.

6. Turn around and leave without looking back. Your wish will come true.

SPELL TO ENSURE A SAFE HOLIDAY

Do this spell on the Wednesday before the person going on holiday is due to leave.

YOU WILL NEED

- 1 red candle
- 1 handful lavender flowers
- 1 handful sage
- ½ handful crushed almonds
- 2 pieces yellow paper
- 2 pieces paui shell (kiwi stone)
- 2 sprigs rosemary
- red ribbon

1. Light the candle and throw the lavender, sage and almonds on a small fire (in a cauldron or outside in the open).

2. Spread out the two pieces of paper and place a piece of shell and a rosemary sprig on each.

3. Fold them into two small packages and tie them with red ribbon. Now pass each package through the smoke as you say:

> Mercury be with me [or whoever's travelling]
> As I travel over land and sea.
> My [or whoever's travelling] safe journey is guaranteed.

4. If you can, mail one of the packages to your destination and leave one at home. If you can't mail one, carry it on your person as you travel.

SPELL TO ENCOURAGE SUNSHINE

You will need

- 1 orange candle
- Suntan lotion
- Carnelian or red jasper crystal

Light the candle, rub suntan lotion into your hands and toss the carnelian or red jasper from palm to palm seven times as you say:

> Goddess Sol, bless and decree
> that the sun shall shine on me.

Do this every morning leading up to your holiday or event you want sunshine for.

SPELL TO ENSURE GOOD FISHING

You will need

- Nettle
- Cinquefoil (five-finger grass)
- Leek

1. Chop and mix a handful of each ingredient then steep in a saucepan of hot (not boiling) water for 10 minutes. Strain the potion and set aside.

2. On the morning you are going fishing, bathe your hands in the potion as you say:

    Fishes of the sea, come to me, come to me.
    Irresistible will I be.
    When I call you from the sea.

3. Take a cup of the potion with you and pour it into the water where you plan to fish as you repeat the charm.

COLD AS A WITCH'S TIT SPELL

Well not really, breasts are usually warm. But if you are cold, here's a spell to warm you up.

1. Cup your left hand gently and focus on a warm ball of red light starting to grow there. As it pulses and fills the palm of your hand, feel it start to travel up your arm, warm and soothing. Now invoke Vulcan, the ancient Roman god of fire:

    Vulcan, bless me with your fire.
    Warm me with your heat and power.

2. Feel the warmth spread swiftly through the rest of your body. Visualise yourself standing engulfed in warm, velvety flames.

3. When you're in a warm place, thank Vulcan and click the fingers of your left hand to switch off the spell.

FOR MORE DESIRABLE COOKING

Put passion into your cooking - get involved! Revel in the sights and scents. With its emphasis on fine tastes and textures, Tuscan cooking is good for romance. Thai cuisine can spice up your love life. (Though garlic breath can be a turn-off! To combat this, chew on some parsley.) To help things along further, say this incantation as you cook:

> *As I weave my new magick*
> *My cooking is no longer tragic.*
> *Tastes and smells entice, enchant,*
> *My fabulous food is not by chance.*

TO IMPROVE MEMORY
FOR SHOPPING LISTS
AND OTHER THINGS

Sip rosemary tea, apply a drop of rosemary essential oil to your temples and say this affirmation:

> *I remember things with ease, extensive is my memory.*

Carry a citrine quartz dabbed with rosemary oil to help enhance your memory. Avoid too much alcohol and coffee - they can dull the memory. (Coffee can stimulate the mind in small amounts, but too much can addle it.)

TO FIND A LOST BRACELET

Write a clear description of the bracelet on a piece of paper. Roll it up, tie a piece of string around the centre and hold the other end of the string in your hand. Concentrate on wearing the bracelet again and having it in your possession as you draw the string slowly towards you saying:

Return to me, return to me.
No longer lost, mine to be.

Chant this over and over, picturing the bracelet returning to you. As you unleash your inner wisdom, a vision could flash before you of where the bracelet is or you may find it in the coming hours.

SPELL TO STOP SOMEONE FROM STEALING

Do this spell on a Saturday, which is ruled by Saturn and good for justice spells.

You will need
- 1 black candle
- Pin, for carving
- Sea salt
- 1 cup olive oil
- Knife, for carving
- Candle holder

1. Carve the person's name on the candle using the pin. If you don't know their name, carve the word 'thief'.

2. Mix a good handful of salt with the olive oil and let the candle soak in it for 3 hours.

3. Remove the candle from the oil, wipe it down and carve out the bottom to expose the wick. Stand the candle on its head and light the bottom wick. As you gaze at the flame, concentrate and say:

Thief, your deeds are no longer tolerated.
It's time for you to stop this behaviour.
By my will, your crimes shall cease
And restore in all a sense of peace.

4. Let the candle burn out. If you can, bury the stub near where the person lives or where they most commonly commit their crime. Otherwise bury it under a tree.

A SPELL FOR SUCCESS IN LEGAL MATTERS AND TO GUARANTEE JUSTICE

You will need

- 1 orange candle
- Orange essential oil
- 8 marigold flowers
- Pinch of dragon's blood powder
- Tiger's eye crystal
- Orange cloth pouch

1. At noon on a Saturday under the sun, anoint the candle with 8 drops orange oil and light it. Place the remaining ingredients into the pouch, then hold the pouch to your heart and invoke Maat, the ancient Egyptian goddess of law and justice:
    Goddess Maat
    with an honest heart,
    I ask you to bless my charm.

2. Thank the goddess, snuff the candle and carry the pouch with you at all times. After doing this spell, things should improve quickly. But if the going is still rough, light the candle again every day at noon. Holding the charm to your heart, ask Maat for her blessings.

Remember, this spell will bring you justice so hopefully you deserve everything to go your way. If you don't, the action of this spell will give you your just desserts.

TO GET BACK A STOLEN CAR OR OTHER STOLEN OR LOST PROPERTY

You will need

- Piece of yellow paper
- Orange pencil, Texta or crayon
- Magnet
- 3 bay leaves (for honesty and truth)
- 3 pinches of cayenne pepper (for speed)
- Long piece of string

1. On the paper, write what you have lost using the orange pencil and place the magnet, bay leaves and cayenne on top. Fold the paper and tie the string around it, leaving a long dangling piece.

2. Sit at a table and place the bundle on the opposite side from you. Holding the end of the string in your right hand, slowly draw it towards you, winding it around your left fist as you say:

    Return to me, my property.
    For the good of all
    So mote it be.

3. Keep the bundle with you (place it in a bag if necessary) until your property is returned or found or a replacement becomes available. When this happens, bury the bundle giving thanks for the bounty of the universe to right the wrongs in the world.

TO HELP KEEP COOL DURING TRAFFIC JAMS

Hang a sprig of lavender bound with gold ribbon from your rear-view mirror. When you are feeling agitated, rub the lavender between your fingers and let the soothing smell calm you. Gold represents having an abundance of patience.

Here are some other ideas:

Visualisation spell

Close your eyes and visualise your car growing wings. Your magickal flying vehicle soars into the sky, gliding smoothly over the cars below. Envision yourself arriving at your destination effortlessly and on time, feeling calm and serene. You may even find the traffic will start moving faster when you do this.

Incantation for patience

Repeat a calming mantra or incantation to yourself, such as:

> *As cars stand still, I keep my calm,*
> *Patience is my soothing balm.*
> *Amidst the chaos, I am grace,*
> *In this jam is my peaceful place.*

Focus on the rhythm of your breath as you say the words, letting them ease your tension.

Traffic jam protection spell

Carry a small charm or talisman in your car that symbolises protection and safety, such as a crystal or a small figurine of a guardian animal. Hold the charm in your hand and imbue it with the intention of keeping you safe and calm while stuck in traffic.

Magickal playlist

Create a playlist of calming and uplifting music to listen to while you're stuck in traffic. Choose songs that soothe your nerves and lift your spirits, transporting you to a magickal realm where traffic jams are but a minor inconvenience on your journey and you arrive on time every time with your sanity intact.

CAR AMULET

Make this amulet to help protect against mechanical problems. The best time to make your amulet is during the waxing to full moon, preferably on a Sunday (ruled by the Sun).

You will need

- Sage leaves (for wisdom)
- 3 black peppercorns (for enthusiasm)
- Piece of turquoise (for warding away trouble)
- 2 iron nails crossed and bound with red thread
- Pale blue pouch

Place all the items in the pouch as you invoke Ra, the ancient Egyptian sun god:

Sun god Ra,
Bless my car
With ease and comfort
Near and far.
May it travel
Sun god Ra.

Hang the amulet inside the car engine or place under the driver's seat.

TO FIND A CARPARK

Visualisation is important so instead of thinking *I'll never find a park* as you head out in the car, just know that you will. Remain calm and clear, allowing your will to shape events around you. Start at the beginning of your trip, picturing everything flowing smoothly and effortlessly. If you want extra help, say this charm:

> *In time and space, I find my car place.*

PROTECTIVE TYRE PAINT

YOU WILL NEED

- 1 tablespoon benzoin (buy at the chemist/drugstore)
- Bucket filled with 3 litres water
- 9 bay laurel leaves
- Brush

1. This is best concocted during the waxing moon. Stir the benzoin into the water and float the bay leaves in it overnight.

2. The following morning, paint your car tyres with the protective paint. Paint this methodically and carefully as you chant:

> *Sacred herb of protection,*
> *Bestow safe travel in all directions.*

3. Repeat this ritual every morning before you drive to your destination.

GAMBLING RITUAL

YOU WILL NEED

- 1 green candle
- Sandalwood essential oil
- Piece of parchment (or paper)

1. Starting Thursday as the moon waxes, anoint the candle with the sandalwood oil and visualise winning. Write your chosen game on the paper as you say: 'I am a winner.'

2. Burn the paper in the candle flame to empower it with the catalyst energy of fire.

3. Let the candle burn for an hour, then snuff it, place it in your left pocket and head to the casino! Finger the candle stub with your left hand and dab a bit of oil from the candle onto items used in the game - chips, cards, tickets, whatever. Keep visualising winning.

SPELL TO HELP A FOOTBALL TEAM WIN AFTER A LOT OF LOSSES

THE TEAM WILL NEED
- Red helium balloons

1. Direct the football team to stand together in a line on the cliff, each holding a red balloon in their right hand. Together as one, they turn sunwise (clockwise in the northern hemisphere, anticlockwise in the southern hemisphere) seven times then face the ocean. They call out with voices united:
   By the power of our team spirit, on the field we will stand strong.
   On the board with the highest score is where we belong.
   With every pass and every kick, we claim our rightful place,
   Together we rise, together we fight, our triumph we embrace!

2. As they do this, they release the red balloons, watching them float into the sky and knowing that winning times lie ahead.

Note: releasing red balloons to float over the ocean pollutes it. A better option is to stand on the cliff into the wind (to change from defeat and invoke good fortune) and hold up red streamers. Once the spell is cast, the team ties the streamers to the foot of their beds so they will walk, run and kick their way to victory.

SPELL TO HELP YOUR FAVOURITE INJURED SPORTING PERSONALITY RETURN TO THE COURT OR FIELD

You will need

- Cornflower
- Water
- 1 blue candle
- 1 pinch cardamon
- 1 pinch cinnamon
- 1 pinch cumin

1. Create a three-herb healing and empowerment candle. Mix cornflour and water into a paste and rub over the blue candle. While the surface is sticky, sprinkle with the cardamon, cinnamon and cumin (all herbs of the sun that are imbued with powerful strengthening forces aligned with sporting energies).

2. Picture your player strong and playing well - even winning! Light the candle and intone:

    I summon my powers of healing thought.
    So that [name of sportsperson] will be back on the court.

3. Feel free to make a rhyme that reflects your magickal intent. When your vision is clear say loudly:

    By the power of three
    So mote it be!

4. Clapping your hands three times, count: 'One, two, three!' Pinch out the flame of the candle; the spell is done.

Note: Rhyming is important when casting spells, because poetry is magickal. So if your player needs to get back on the field rather than the court, say this at step 2:

With healing will I decree,
That [name of sportsperson] will get back on the field.

EGYPTIAN SPELLS

In the year I edited the *Lost Book of Spells*, I was living in Egypt. I spent a lot of time in the sites of sacred antiquities and was inspired to create spells based on the wisdom depicted in the tombs and the extraordinary energies suffusing there.

Ritual for blessing by the goddess Hathor

This ritual is to honour your life and death. It asks for the goddess Hathor's blessings and assistance in this world and the next.

YOU WILL NEED

- 1 white candle
- Sand or soil from a sacred place (somewhere you feel a sense of reverence for the gift of life)
- Blend of myrrh and frankincense or floral jasmine incense
- Statue or image of Hathor or a cow (a symbol of Hathor)
- Small bowl
- Organic milk
- Cosmetics or cosmetic-related items as offerings (optional)
- Scent offering (a lush blend of essential oils or your favourite perfume)

1. Create a sacred space where you can perform the ritual undisturbed. Place the white candle in the centre of your space, surrounded by the sacred sand or soil. Light the incense.
2. Position the representation of Hathor facing the candle.
3. Fill the small bowl with milk and place it next to the candle.

4. Arrange cosmetics as offerings, which symbolise reverence and devotion to Hathor's role as goddess of beauty. The ancient Egyptians made offerings in little alabaster urns of kohl, scents of oils, honey and resins. If using perfume in a spray bottle, spray it above your offerings to further communicate your adoration to Hathor.

PART 1: INVOCATION AND OFFERINGS

1. Light the white candle, symbolising purity and divine light. Close your eyes and take a few deep breaths to centre yourself. Honour the presence of the goddess Hathor with sincerity and reverence.

2. Recite the following invocation or adapt it to your own words:

   Great goddess Hathor, beloved of Egypt,
   Lady of love, beauty and joy
   And protector of women and men alike,
   I recognise thee with reverence and adoration.

3. Offer prayers in your own words of gratitude to Hathor, acknowledging her multifaceted nature and divine influence in your life. Present offerings of cosmetics, symbolising reverence and devotion to Hathor's role as the goddess of beauty.

4. Meditate on the blessings of your life, thinking of good, sustainable, regenerative experiences and feelings.

5. Give gratitude to Hathor again by repeating the charm and anointing your pulse points with the scent offering to further align with her energies.

PART 2: CONNECTION TO THE AFTERLIFE AND BLESSINGS

1. Reflect upon the scenes depicted in the ancient Egyptian tombs, such as Pharoah Ay and Hatshepsut's mortuary temple, which show the deceased being welcomed by Hathor's loving embrace.

2. Visualise yourself in the presence of Hathor, feeling her nurturing and protective energy surrounding you.

3. State your intentions clearly and respectfully, asking Hathor for her blessings to be bestowed upon you for the rest of your life and beyond. You may use the following words or modify them as you need:

   Goddess Hathor, source of love and joy,
   Bless me with your radiant light.
   Grant me health, fertility and inner harmony in this life
   So I may shine in the eyes of others and offer them the gifts you have bestowed upon me.
   May I then walk in beauty and grace from this world to the next into your loving embrace.

4. Anoint yourself with the scented offering.

PART 3: CLOSING

1. In your own words, express gratitude to Hathor for her presence and blessings. Snuff the candle, symbolising the completion of the ritual.

2. Leave the representation of Hathor in its place as a symbol of ongoing connection and reverence.

PART 4: CONTINUED CONNECTION

Whenever you seek guidance or reassurance, return to this sacred space and reconnect with Hathor's energy through meditation, prayer or offerings.

UNIQUE MEXICAN SPELLS

In 2020, I spent two months in Mexico meditating and participating in sober Temescal ceremonies, giving me a fascinating glimpse into the world of female magical practitioners, called *brujas* or *curanderas*. While the following spells come from the original spell book, now I've spent time on the land where they originated and with the women who perform them, they carry even greater magical weight.

The bruja's magical practices are a beguiling blend of indigenous beliefs, Spanish influences and African elements. Brujas have a profound knowledge of healing herbs, spiritual cleansing and protective spells. Their practices revolve around the sacred use of plants, devout ceremonies and the invocation of spirits to restore balance and harmony. And the community's respect of them is absolute.

Mexican healing spell

YOU WILL NEED

- 1 whole egg
- Glass of water
- Peppertree or eucalyptus branches
- Rue
- Fresh flowers
- Cigarette

1. Rub the patient with an unbroken egg to absorb their illness. Then break the egg into a glass of water and use your divination skills to determine the illness.

2. Make a bundle of peppertree or eucalyptus branches, rue and fresh flowers. Focus on releasing the illness as you brush the bundle over the patient to erase the evil *aire* (aura) of the illness.

3. Blow cigarette smoke on the patient to prevent the escaping *aire* from infecting others.

4. Put the person to bed for one day to sleep off the escaping illness.

EGG DIVINATION

CLEAR AND UNBROKEN YOLK	Good health; no significant issues are present.
CLOUDY EGG WHITE	Presence of negative energy or minor physical ailments; spiritual cleansing may be needed.
BUBBLES OR FOAM	Indicates stress, anxiety or emotional turmoil; emotional or mental healing is needed.
BLOOD SPOTS	Possible serious illness or physical ailment that requires immediate attention; seek medical advice.
FIGURES OR FACES	Spirits or ancestors are trying to communicate; important messages or warnings should be heeded.
THREADS OR STRANDS	Presence of spiritual ties or attachments; spiritual detachment or protection may be needed.
EYE SHAPE	Evil eye or envy is directed towards the person; protective measures against mal de ojo, or 'evil eye' are recommended.
SPIDER WEB PATTERN	Entrapment or being caught in a problematic situation; suggests the need for breaking free or protection.

FRIGHT SPELL

Mexicans believe that if you have a bad fright, your soul escapes from your body and wanders the astral plane until the curing rite is performed. A fright can be an argument, car accident, illness or curse.

You will need
- Bowl of water
- Fresh seasonal flowers (for healing)

1. At noon under the midday sun, the person with the fright holds a bowl of water into which the witch throws healing flowers while focusing on finding the person's lost soul.
2. On the stroke of 12, she shouts the person's name three times to call back the lost soul.
3. The person takes three mouthfuls of water. Their soul has returned and they are healed. They pour the remaining water on the ground as an offering.

This spell is especially good if you or someone has been cursed by the evil eye.

If you are having trouble courting a girl

Carry a dead hummingbird in your pocket (!)

To seduce a girl

Put the leg of a beetle in her glass of soft drink. This will make her desire sex (!)

To control a misbehaving husband

While your husband sleeps, measure his body with a red ribbon (stretch it out from the top of his head to his toes). Wrap the ribbon around a large black candle and burn it upside down (flip the candle, expose the wick and light). Leave the candle burning beside him while he sleeps. His bad behaviour will be gone on waking.

GROUP RITUAL OF GRATITUDE

In a world often shadowed by trials and losses, certain souls have a profound resilience - those who, despite their hardships, radiate gratitude and compassion. This ritual is dedicated to celebrating those individuals whose unwavering spirit transforms adversity into strength and abundance. To perform this ritual, create a comfortable, serene space adorned with candles or soft lighting.

You WILL NEED

- Candles
- Purification oil (see box on page 252)
- Incense or sage
- Journal or piece of paper
- Symbols of nature such as flowers or stones (for grounding gifts)

1. Create a tranquil sacred energy in your chosen ceremonial space. Anoint the candles with your purification oil then light them. To further purify the space, burn incense or sage to release cluttered energy and invite in clear, positive energy. Take a few deep breaths to centre yourself and set your intention for the ritual, which is to honour those who show and share gratitude in the face of hardship and loss.

2. Sit comfortably with the journal or paper and pen. Invite the individual for whom this ritual is intended to join you if possible. Reflect on the challenges and losses they have

endured, acknowledging the depth of their journey. Encourage them to write down these experiences, allowing space for any emotions that arise. If the person cannot attend, write down your interpretation of them and their strength, humility and resilience that inspire you and the group.

3. Transition into a gratitude meditation, shifting the group's focus towards blessings and strengths. Guide the group to close their eyes; take slow, deep breaths; and visualise a warm, golden light surrounding them. With each inhale, invite them to draw in gratitude for the simple joys and moments of connection they have experienced despite their own challenges. With each exhale, encourage them to release any lingering pain or sorrow.

4. With newfound gratitude filling their hearts, guide the group in reciting affirmations that emphasise their resilience, strength and capacity to give back to the world. Encourage them to speak these affirmations aloud with conviction, reinforcing their belief in their ability to create positive change.

5. Invite the group to consider the ways in which they can share their blessings with others, no matter how small. Whether it's a kind gesture, supportive word or helping hand, encourage them to recognise the profound impact of their actions on those around them. They may choose to write down their intentions or simply hold them in their heart.

6. As a symbolic gesture of renewal and abundance, offer each group member a natural object such as a flower or stone. Encourage them to imbue this symbol with their intentions for a joyful and sustainable life, infusing it with the energy of gratitude and empowerment.

7. Conclude the ritual with a moment of silent reflection. Allow everyone to bask in the warmth of gratitude and promise of a brighter future when fuelled with gratitude and selfless giving. Encourage each person to turn to their neighbour and express

their appreciation for each other's presence and resilience, affirming everyone's journey towards abundance and joy.

8. Encourage each person to carry this energy of gratitude and empowerment with them beyond the ritual, integrating it into their daily lives. Suggest revisiting their affirmations and intentions regularly, cultivating a mindset of abundance and generosity - for in the alchemy of gratitude and resili ere is transformative power that transcends adversity and ces a sustainable life of abundance and joy.

HOW TO BLEND A PURIFICATION OIL

INGREDIENTS

- Small glass bottle or container
- ¼ cup carrier oil (jojoba, almond or unscented coconut oil)
- 5 drops sage essential oil
- 5 drops cedarwood essential oil
- 3 drops lemon essential oil
- 3 drops lavender essential oil

1. In the small glass bottle, pour the carrier oil. Add the drops of each essential oil. Close the bottle tightly and swirl gently to blend the oils.
2. Allow the mixture to sit for a day to let the scents and energies meld. Use this purification oil during rituals, spells or ceremonies by anointing candles, tools or yourself to cleanse and purify the energy within and around you.

EARTH HEALING RITUAL: LIVING IN SUSTAINABLE HARMONY

This ritual is designed to channel healing energy to the earth, fostering your deeper connection with nature and promoting sustainable behaviours that benefit the planet. In the 20-plus years since I first collated this spell book, life on the planet has changed. Our human impact is often not holistic or sustainable. This ritual seeks to address that imbalance and promote conscious healing and appreciation for the earth.

YOU WILL NEED

- Items to create a sacred space (optional)
- Candle
- Pine or frankincense incense
- Clear quartz crystal (or any stone that resonates with healing energy)
- Small pouch or container filled with native plant or wildflower seeds
- Small piece of biodegradable paper
- Pencil
- Bowl of pure water

1. Find a quiet outdoor space where you feel a strong connection to nature. Set up your ritual space, arranging the items in a way that feels harmonious to you. Take a few moments to ground yourself, feeling your connection to the earth beneath your feet while your crown chakra opens to the sky as a conduit for positive renewable universal energy.

2. Light a candle and some earthy green incense then take a few deep breaths to centre yourself. Hold the clear quartz crystal in your dominant hand and visualise it glowing and pulsing with bright, healing energy. Set your intention to send healing energy to the earth and cultivate sustainable behaviours in your everyday life.

3. Take the pouch of seeds and hold it in your hands. Visualise each seed as a symbol of positive change and renewal for the earth. As you scatter the seeds onto the ground, recite a simple affirmation such as:

With each seed I sow, I nurture the earth's growth and healing.

4. Take the paper and pencil. Write down one practical, sustainable behaviour you commit to incorporating into your daily life to benefit the planet. It could be reducing plastic use, conserving water or supporting local businesses. Fold the paper gently and hold it to your heart, infusing it with love and intention.

5. Dip your fingers into the bowl of water and sprinkle a few drops onto the ground as an offering to the earth. With each drop, visualise a ripple of healing energy spreading outwards, nurturing the land and all living beings.

6. Sit quietly in meditation, focusing on your breath and the natural world around you. Feel the energy of the earth flowing through you, filling you with a sense of peace and renewal. Express gratitude for the beauty and abundance of the planet with your thoughts and sense of appreciation. If it is a private place and you feel inclined, speak aloud your prayers and statements of gratitude and love.

7. When you feel ready, offer thanks to the earth and all the elements for their presence and support. Release any remaining energy into the earth by pressing both your hands into it, knowing it will be absorbed and utilised for healing and growth. Gently extinguish the candles and incense and pack away your ritual items.

8. Carry the intention you wrote on the biodegradable paper with you as a reminder of your commitment to sustainable living. Look for opportunities in your daily life to practise eco-friendly behaviours and continue nurturing your connection with the earth. You can also carry the crystal with you to further magnify your intentions.

FURTHER THOUGHTS

Instead of scattering the seeds, consider planting them into the soil of the location - if that is appropriate - and water them when you come to the water offering part of the ritual. Consider burying the crystal with the seeds you plant to further give back healing energy and gratitude to our great Mother Earth.

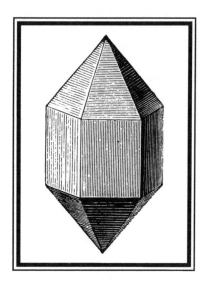

GLOSSARY
OF
INGREDIENTS

Witchy ingredients and where to find them.

INGREDIENT	WHAT IT IS AND WHAT IT'S USED FOR
Betony	Betony has protective properties, warding off evil spirits and negative energies. You can plant it around your home or carry it as an amulet for protection. Betony enhances clarity of mind - it can dispel nightmares and promote restful sleep.
Borage blossoms	Courage and bravery. Carrying borage flowers or drinking borage tea can lift the spirits and instil confidence and optimism. It has protective qualities, warding off evil and negativity. Use it in love and healing spells to bring comfort and joy.
Buckbean	Use buckbean to ward off evil spirits, enhance vitality, and purify spaces and individuals from negative energies.
Cedarwood	With its protective and purifying properties, use cedarwood to ward off evil spirits, attract positive energy and promote spiritual clarity.
Cinquefoil leaves	Good luck, protection and prosperity. Use cinquefoil in charms and rituals to attract positive outcomes and ward off negativity.
Coltsfoot	Protective and healing properties. Coltsfoot is often used to ward off illness, soothe coughs and promote overall respiratory health.
Cowslip	Use protective and love-enhancing cowslip in charms and potions to attract love and ensure good fortune.
Damiana tea	Aphrodisiac and mood-enhancing damiana tea is used in love spells to promote emotional well-being.
Dragon's blood powder	Protective and purifying properties. Use it to ward off negative energies and enhance spell work.
Elderwood	Protective and healing properties. Elderwood promotes health and well-being.
Eyebright	Vision-enhancing and healing properties. Eyebright improves eyesight and treats eye-related ailments.
Frankincense resin	Purifying and spiritual properties. Frankincense cleanses spaces, enhances meditation and promotes connection with the divine.
Hops	Calming and sleep-inducing. Use hops in pillows and teas to promote restful sleep and ward off nightmares.

Well-stocked herbal shops and garden centres. Betony grows wild in meadows, woodlands and grassy areas across Europe and parts of Asia and North America.

Garden centres, nurseries, health-food shops and online. While borage is native to the Mediterranean, it can now be foraged in Europe, North America and other temperate climates.

Herbal shops and online. You can forage buckbean in wetlands, marshes, and along pond and stream edges in temperate regions of the northern hemisphere.

Herbal and aromatherapy shops and online. You can forage cedarwood in forests and wooded areas where cedar trees naturally grow.

Herbal shops and online. Cinquefoil can be found growing in meadows and fields and along roadsides in temperate regions.

Health-food and herbal shops. You can forage coltsfoot from damp, shaded areas such as stream banks and roadsides worldwide.

Herbal and health-food shops and online. Cowslip can be foraged in open meadows and grassy areas throughout Europe and parts of Asia.

Herbal and health-food shops and online. You can source damiana indigenously from Central and South America.

Herbal and metaphysical shops and online. Dragon's blood powder comes from the resin of certain tree species in tropical regions of Southeast Asia.

Herbal and woodworking shops. This wood is sourced from elder trees commonly found in woodlands and hedgerows in temperate regions.

Herbal shops and online. You find eyebright growing in meadows and grassy areas in Europe and North America.

Herbal and aromatherapy shops and online. Frankincense comes from the resin of *Boswellia* trees from the Arabian Peninsula, northeast Africa and India.

Herbal and brewing supply shops and online. Hops is cultivated in temperate regions such as Europe, North America and parts of Asia.

INGREDIENT	WHAT IT IS AND WHAT IT'S USED FOR
Mandrake root	Famed for its magical and protective properties, mandrake is used in powerful spells for protection and attracting love.
Mugwort	Revered for its protective and visionary properties, mugwort enhances dreams, provides protection and aids in divination.
Myrrh	Esteemed for its protective and purifying qualities, myrrh cleanses spaces, promotes healing and enhances spiritual practices.
Orris root	Love-drawing and protection. Use orris root in sachets and spells to attract romance and ward off negative influences.
Patchouli	Grounding and prosperity. Patchouli draws wealth, enhances sensuality and promotes spiritual growth.
Sandalwood powder	Purifying and calming. Sandalwood promotes spiritual clarity, attracts positive energies and enhances meditation practices.
Senna powder	Purgative and cleansing. Senna purifies the body and spirit, promoting overall well-being and renewal.
St John's wort leaves	Protective and healing. St John's wort wards off evil, enhances mood, and promotes overall health and well-being. It was traditionally gathered on Midsummer's Eve and hung in homes to protect against lightning, fire and malevolent forces.
Tumbleweed	Symbol of desolation and wandering. Tumbleweed represents the restless, transient nature of life. Use it to encourage someone to 'blow away.'
Uva ursi leaves	Also known as bearberry, uva ursi has protective and healing properties. Use it to ward off negative energies and promote urinary health and well-being.
Vervain	Protective and healing, vervain attracts love, repels evil, and promotes peace and prosperity.
Willowbark	Healing and pain-relieving, willowbark reduces fever, alleviates pain, and promotes overall health and well-being.
Witch's broom	Associated with magical flight, protection and housecleaning rituals, witch's broom symbolises the ability to sweep away negative energies and bring good fortune.
Yarrow	Protective and healing. Yarrow promotes courage and aids in divination and love spells.

WHERE TO FIND IT
Herbal shops and online. Mandrake is native to the Mediterranean region and parts of southern Europe.
Herbal and health-food shops and online. You can forage mugwort in fields and along roadsides across Europe, Asia and North America.
Herbal and aromatherapy shops and online. Myrrh comes from the resin of *Commiphora* trees found in arid regions of northeast Africa and the Arabian Peninsula.
Herbal and specialty spice shops and online. Orris root comes from the rhizomes of the *Iris germanica* or *I. pallida* plants, cultivated in Italy and Morocco.
Herbal and aromatherapy shops and online. Patchouli comes from the leaves of the patchouli plant, cultivated in tropical regions of Southeast Asia.
Herbal and aromatherapy shops and online. The powder comes from the heartwood of sandalwood trees, grown in regions such as India, Australia and Southeast Asia.
Herbal and health-food shops and online. Senna powder comes from the leaves and pods of senna plants, grown in northern Africa, the Middle East and parts of India.
Herbal and health-food shops and online. You can forage St Joh's wort in sunny, open areas such as meadows, fields and roadsides, in temperate regions across Europe, North America and Asia.
You can forage tumbleweed in arid and semi-arid regions, particularly in western USA where it's common in open fields and deserts, and along roadsides. Not typically sold commercially, but you can sometimes find dried tumbleweeds through specialty decor shops or online.
Herbal and health-food shops and online. You can forage uva ursi in dry, rocky areas and open woodlands across North America, Europe and Asia.
Herbal and health-food shops and online. You can forage vervain in sunny, well-drained areas such as meadows, fields and roadsides in temperate regions across Europe, North America and Asia.
Herbal and health-food shops and online. You can forage the bark of willow trees, which are found near rivers, streams and wetlands across Europe, North America and Asia.
Metaphysical and witchcraft supply shops and online. You can make your own broom from materials such as an ash- or birchwood handle and birch twigs, found in woodlands and rural areas. Or use straw.
Herbal and health-food shops and online. You can forage yarrow in meadows and fields, and along roadsides in temperate regions across Europe, North America and Asia.

WILD FORAGING

Some tips when foraging for herbs and plants in the wild:

- Identify the plant correctly to avoid any toxic look-alikes.
- Forage in areas free from pesticides, herbicides and pollutants.
- Seek permission if foraging on private property.
- Harvest sustainably, taking only what you need and leaving plenty for wildlife and future growth.

BE ETHICAL AND SUSTAINABLE WHEN SOURCING YOUR SUPPLIES

Patronise reputable herbal and metaphysical shops IRL and online, which can give you detailed information about their sources. Some trees from which the resin is harvested for dragon's blood powder, such as *Dracaena*, *Daemonorops* and *Croton* species, are endangered due to overharvesting and habitat destruction. But you can now source dragon's blood from the Indonesian rattan palm - the unripe fruit produces red resin. This is a sustainable and better choice.

ABOUT THE AUTHOR

Fiona Horne is one of the world's most respected witches. She is the author of 15 bestselling books on modern witchcraft, published over the last two decades, that see her work having a generational impact on the evolution of the modern witch. Her tireless devotion to dispelling negative myths and stereotypes has contributed to the freedom that modern witches have in practising their craft without fearing vilification and persecution.

Thirty years ago Fiona launched a career in the entertainment industry as the lead singer of the chart-topping Aussie electro-rock band Def FX. In 1997 she released her first book, *Witch - A Personal Journey*, with Random House and became a popular television and radio personality, appearing on many programs globally.

Based in Los Angeles from 2001 to 2013, in addition to her many published books, Fiona scored prime-time TV as 'The Witch' on SyFy channel's hit reality show *Mad Mad House* and was invited to speak at Harvard University on witchcraft in modern media.

Moving to the Caribbean in 2013, Fiona worked as a commercial pilot and volunteered in humanitarian and animal aid. In 2017 she returned to publishing with her autobiography *The Naked Witch*, followed by 2019's manifesto *The Art of Witch* and 2021's *Teen Magick: Witchcraft for a New Generation*. Fiona also released her debut oracle deck *The Magick of You* to acclaim in 2019, followed by 2023's *Dark Magick*, and 2024's *Lost Oracle*.

In recent times Fiona continues to inspire. With a guitar in her hand, she created a successful rock band project, *SEAWITCH* 2020-2023 with a number 2 Australian indie rock chart album debut, *Well of Spells*. Her '90s band Def FX continues to enjoy sold-out reunion tours in Australia.

In 2024, Fiona relocated to Egypt to curate nourishing spiritual adventures for women, called *Meet Yourself in Egypt*. Combining her passion and expertise for travel and adventure, as well as her magickal skills and experience, these culturally respectful deep dives into the spiritual core of this most magnificent of ancient lands offer women a profound life expanding rebirth.

Fiona is following her calling and now offering her curated bespoke adventures in Bali. And more in Egypt after her first two sold out MYiE of 2024.

For more information and opportunities to join, visit Fiona's website - fionahorne.com

Her personal passions include being a 100 foot+ freediver, world record-holding skydiver, professional fire dancer, and avid student of ancient herstory and magickal traditions.

fionahorne.com | ⓞ captainfifi | f fionahorneofficial